# MAKING
# INVENTIVE WOODEN
# T⚙⚙YS

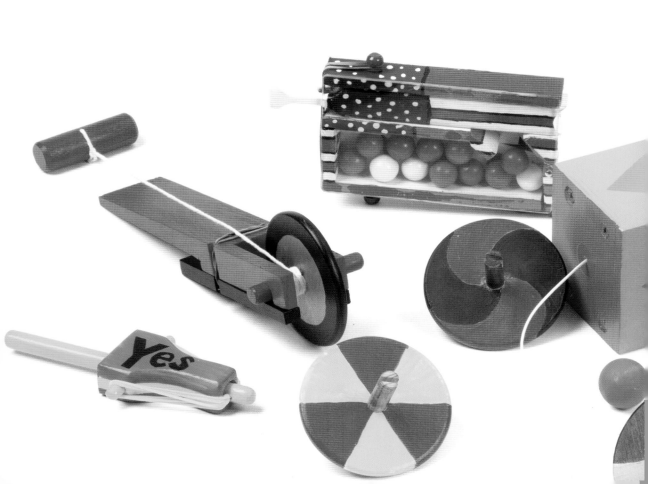

# MAKING INVENTIVE WOODEN TOYS

## 33 Wild & Wacky Projects
## Ideal for STEAM Education

**BOB GILSDORF**

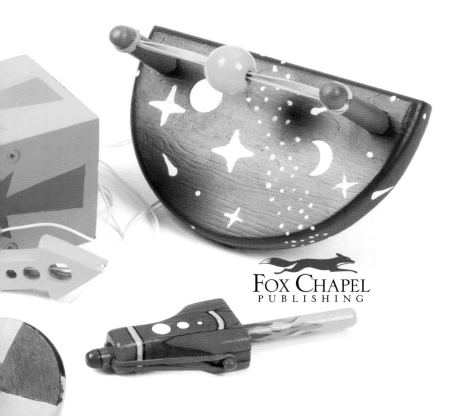

FOX CHAPEL
PUBLISHING

## DON'T SHOOT PEOPLE OR ANIMALS.

There are many toys in this book that launch objects through the air or shoot objects across the ground. Be extremely careful not to aim at any people or animals. If your want to aim at something, line up some action figures or empty cans.

Shutterstock credits: (Visual Generation: **pages 162** bottom, **165** bottom)

ISBN 978-1-56523-948-7

Library of Congress Cataloging-in-Publication Data

Names: Gilsdorf, Bob, 1963- author.
Title: Making inventive wooden toys / by Bob Gilsdorf.
Description: Mount Joy, PA : Fox Chapel Publishing Company, [2018] | Includes index.
Identifiers: LCCN 2018028322 (print) | LCCN 2018030117 (ebook) | ISBN 9781607655466 (ebook) | ISBN 9781565239487 (softcover)
Subjects: LCSH: Wooden toy making. | Mechanical toys.
Classification: LCC TT174.5.W6 (ebook) | LCC TT174.5.W6 G548 2018 (print) | DDC 745.592--dc23
LC record available at https://lccn.loc.gov/2018028322

To learn more about the other great books from Fox Chapel Publishing, or to find a retailer near you, call toll-free 800-457-9112 or visit us at *www.FoxChapelPublishing.com.*

We are always looking for talented authors. To submit an idea, please send a brief inquiry to acquisitions@foxchapelpublishing.com.

Printed in Singapore

First printing

# DEDICATION

This book is dedicated to my awesome wife to thank her for all the support, patience, editing, painting, hand-modeling, typing, and loving kindness she gave me to make this book possible. It is also dedicated to my five boys who still continue to inspire me with their ideas and adventures. A special shout-out to Noah for all his work on the exploded diagrams. Finally, this book is dedicated to the next round of kids that are just reaching the toy-maker age.

# CONTENTS

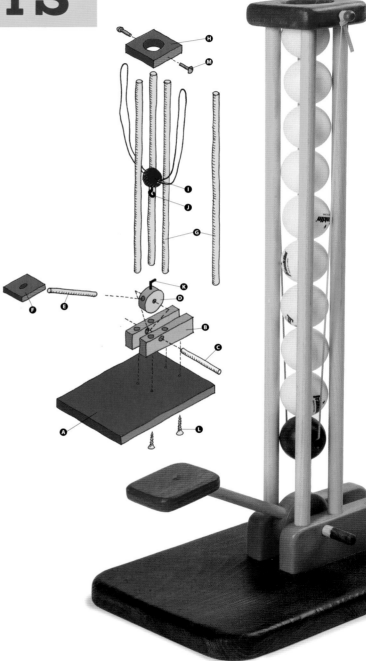

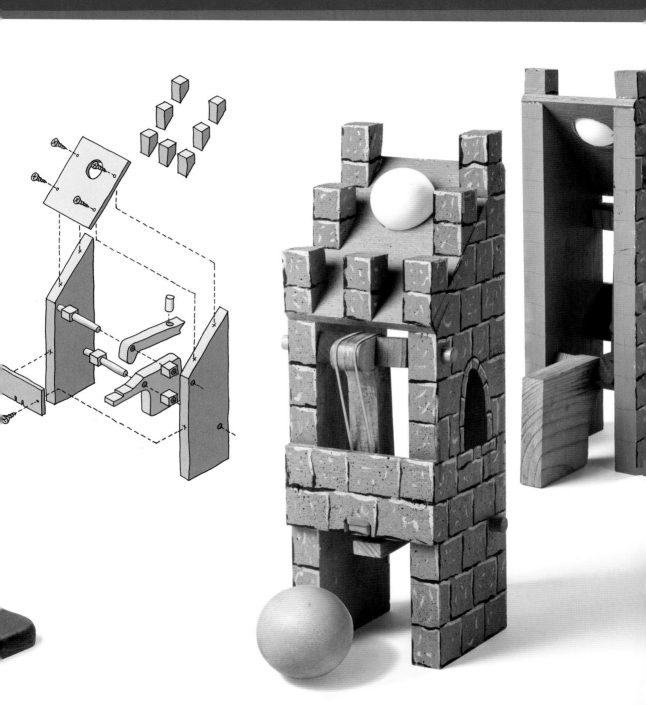

# PREFACE

Have a look at the projects listed in the Contents? Ready to go full steam ahead? Well, there's more! Yes, these are high-octane, exciting, slightly bizarre toys that you build yourself (with some grown-up help to use the power tools), but there is a secret treasure buried deep within each project. However, finding the riches that they hold requires actually making and playing with them. In this book we call it "playing" whereas scientists and engineers call it "experimenting." You have to try out your toy, see what it does, tweak it a little, and observe what happens next. So what treasures will be revealed to the inventor, creator, and maker of each project? These toys each contain real-life lessons in science, technology, engineering, art, and math—aka STEAM.

Science comes to life in these toys, and you actually see the laws of physics right before your eyes. Storing energy sounds mighty complicated, but that's exactly what a rubber band does when it is stretched to launch a catapult or when you wind up a spool of string. Can you store twice the energy with two rubber bands? There's only one way to find out and it's the fun way—just do it! Does stretching a rubber band further store more energy? That will be obvious when you try it. Stretch it too far and it breaks. Now you have an engineering problem to solve. Engineers basically exploit the laws of physics to make and do useful things.

## WARNING: THIS IS NOT YOUR NORMAL PROJECT BOOK!

Inventing toys is a wild, bumpy ride with plenty of experiments and mistakes. For each project, I'm going to share some of the ideas I used to start construction. I'll also show you some challenges (aka major failures!) I faced. But I won't be giving you precise steps explaining exactly how to build each toy. Study the illustrations, learn from mistakes, and keep trying, as all great inventors do. The answer will eventually come, and when it does, yelling "Awesome!" sure feels good. Start creating your own amazing toys!

Build the Top Launcher and you'll learn all about the "conservation of angular momentum" without even having to crack open a physics textbook. A spinning top doesn't sound very high tech until you learn that the exact same principles are used to position satellites in outer space. Of course, engineers like to change the name from "spinning top" to "gyroscope" to sound more impressive.

But let's not get bogged down in all the educational stuff, let's just have fun building, decorating, and discovering what fun we can have when we make something by ourselves. That alone is enough for the laws of physics to be stamped into your minds. Let the making begin!

# DESKTOP ROCKETS

This project was inspired by my mild disappointment with retractable ballpoint pens. Yes, they are ingenious little contraptions with a clever latching mechanism and a spring-loaded button that prevents large ink spots from growing in your pocket. Where's the disappointment? Well, have you ever pushed that button down on a desk and then released the pen? Of course you have, everyone has. The pen hops a disappointing inch or so. The kid in me wants the pen to soar at least several feet in the air to the altitude where my imagination can turn it into something spectacular and sound effects can be added. So that's what I set out to accomplish—a desktop rocket that would gain some serious altitude and ignite a kid's imagination.

## MATERIALS

- ¾" x 1 ½" x 2 ½" (2cm x 4cm x 6cm) pine board (aka a chunk of 1"x2")
- ⅜" (1cm) dowel 5 ½" (14cm) long
- ¼" (6mm) dowel 1 ½" (4cm) long
- #64 3 ½" x ¼" (9cm x 6mm) rubber band

## TOOLS

- Scissors
- Ruler
- Pencil
- Coping saw or scroll saw
- Awl
- Drill with bits: ⅛" (3mm), ¼" (6mm), ½" (13mm)
- 3" (8cm) of thin wire

## SMART ROCKET:

*Let your rocket help you make decisions. Write "Yes" on one side and "No" on the other. Ask your rocket a question and then launch it to get the answer.*

## REVERSE ENGINEERING

First, let's take apart a pen to see what makes it jump. Aha! What we find is a very tiny spring on one side of the ink tube. No wonder it doesn't hop very high.

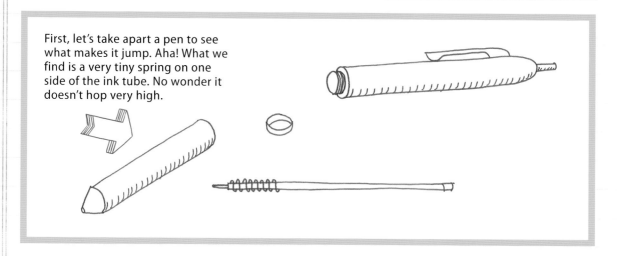

## MORE SPRING

If we want the rocket to go higher we'll need to design something with a larger spring.

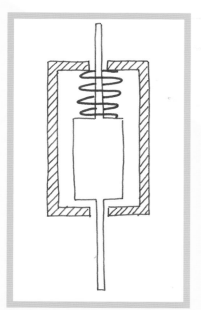

## SIMPLER ROCKET FUEL

The perfect spring can be hard to find. So rather than compressing a spring to store energy, we can simplify our rocket by instead stretching a rubber band. This makes it very easy to experiment with a wide variety of rubber bands.

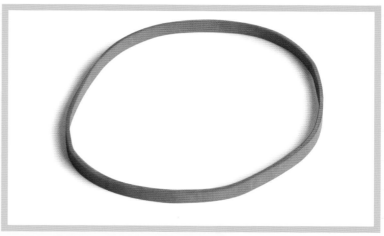

Use your measuring and marking tools to mark the dimensions and locations shown. The grain should run lengthwise down the rocket body. Use an awl to mark the locations of the holes. These small indentations will keep your bit from wandering. Cut the rocket body to the 1½" by 2½" size. Drilling holes in square boards is much easier than drilling holes in weirdly shaped boards. Drill the holes in the rocket body and fuel rod. Use a clamp and a drill press to drill the hole for the fuel rod.

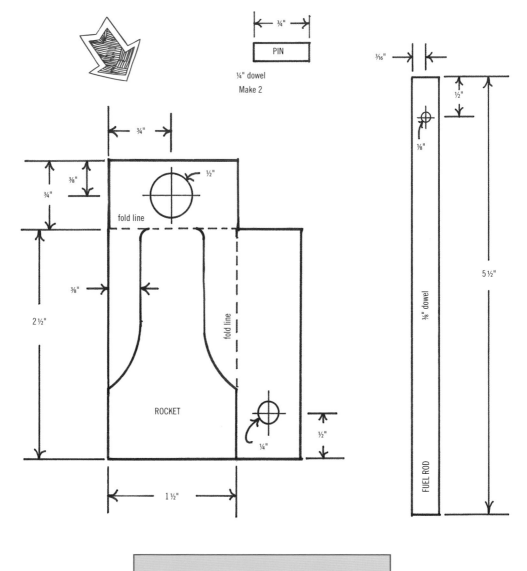

**Note: Patterns are not drawn to scale.**

Insert the pins into the holes in the rocket body. Glue them in place with about ¼" (6mm) protruding from the sides, making sure that neither pin is visible in the hole for the fuel rod.

Pull a rubber band through the hole in the fuel rod. I use a thin wire. Make sure there are equal lengths of rubber band on either side of the fuel rod.

Place the fuel rod into the hole in the rocket body. Make sure the end with the rubber band is at the narrow top of the body. Loop each side of the rubber band around a pin on either side.

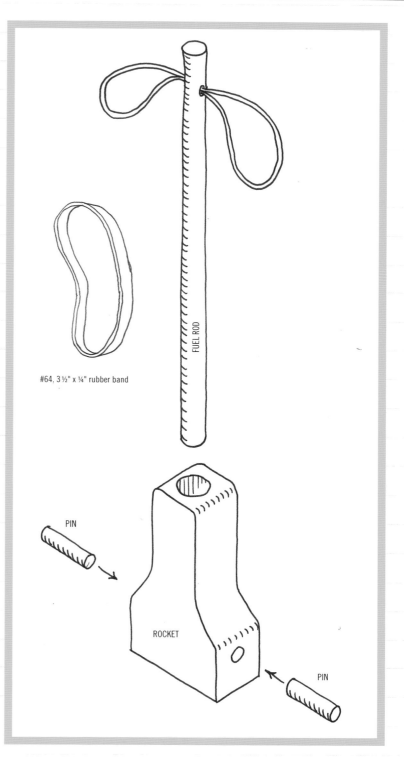

#64, 3 ½" x ¼" rubber band

FUEL ROD

PIN

ROCKET

PIN

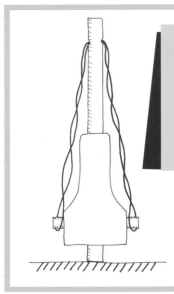

## TEST PILOT

WARNING: Safety always comes first. You don't know how high your rocket will soar, so before launching the rocket be sure there is nothing above you, such as a fluorescent light, ceiling fan, satellite, or (more importantly) any part of you!

## ROCKETS AWAY

Launch the rocket by pinching both sides of the body between your thumb and forefinger. Place the end of the fuel rod on the table and press down on the rocket body until the base of the body is flat on the table surface. Release your fingers and watch your rocket soar. For a higher launch try licking your fingers. After testing the rocket out, sand, shape, and decorate it in a variety of ways.

# DESKTOP ROCKET LAUNCHER

*"Roger, launch team.
We are Go for launch.*

*T-minus 10, 9, 8, 7, 6, 5, 4, Ignition,
2, 1, and lift-off. We have lift-off!"*

**E**very rocket needs a launch pad, even if your rocket fits in the palm of your hand and launches from your desktop like the last project we built. The launch pad is where you will load the fuel, perform last-minute safety checks, strap yourself in, and do the final countdown. Nothing is more exhilarating than releasing the immense power of a rocket with just the tip of your finger. Let's start inventing!

## MATERIALS
- ¾" x 3 ½" x 8 ½"
  (2cm x 9cm x 22cm)
  pine board
- ¾" x 2" x 7"
  (2cm x 5cm x 18cm)
  pine board
- ¾" x ¾" x 3 ½"
  (2cm x 2cm x 9cm) pine board
- 3 – 1 ¼" (3cm) coarse-thread
  drywall screws

## TOOLS
- Drill with bits: ⅛" (3mm),
  ⁵⁄₃₂" (4mm)
- Phillips screwdriver
- Scroll saw
- Tape measure
- Square
- Awl
- Pencil
- Scissors

## HEADS OR TAILS ROCKET:

*Why just flip a coin when you can
launch a rocket?*

# FIGURING IT OUT

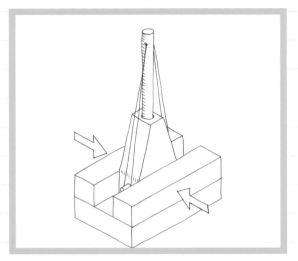

We currently launch our rocket by pinching it between our fingers and releasing it. Let's copy that action and start by holding the rocket between two blocks of wood.

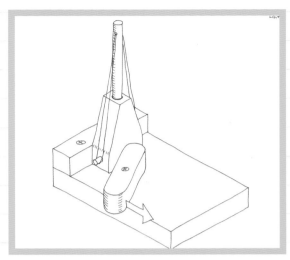

Make one block stationary and turn the other block into a lever to launch the rocket. The problem is that we still have to hold the lever. Hmmm . . .

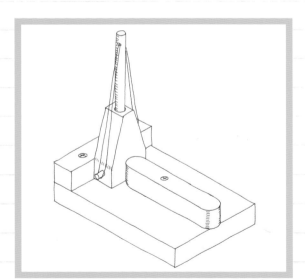

If the lever is just the right size, it will wedge against the rocket and hold it in place. This level of precision, however, will be difficult to build.

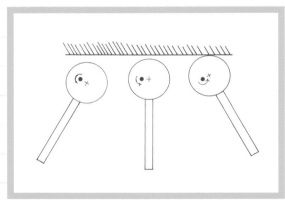

Instead, we can make a clamp that closes the gap as it rotates. This is done by using a circle and rotating around a point that is off-center. Now the rocket is secured until the final launch command is given.

# CREATING THE PARTS

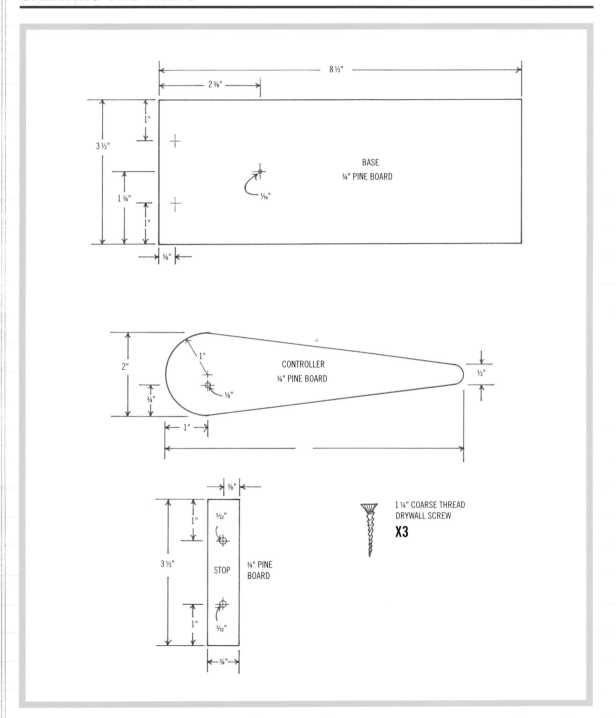

BASE
¾" PINE BOARD

8 ½"

2 ⅜"

1"

3 ½"

1 ¾"

1"

⅜"

1/16"

CONTROLLER
¾" PINE BOARD

2"

1"

¾"

⅛"

1"

½"

STOP

¾" PINE
BOARD

3 ½"

⅜"

1"

5/32"

1"

5/32"

¾"

1 ¼" COARSE THREAD
DRYWALL SCREW

**X3**

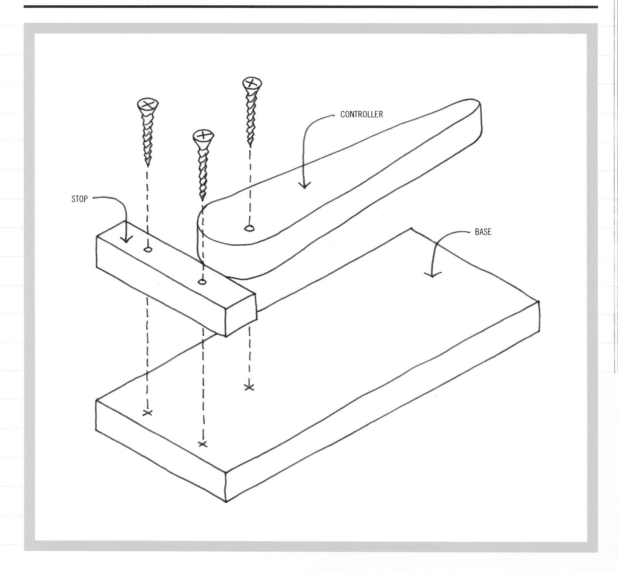

CONTROLLER

STOP

BASE

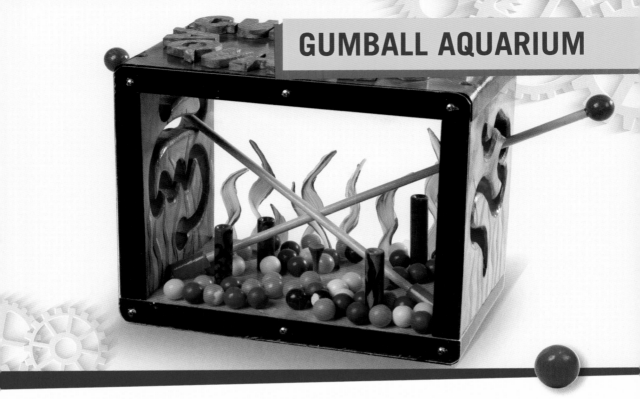

# GUMBALL AQUARIUM

A simple idea for a toy came to mind: to build a gumball machine that requires the would-be-bubble-blower to demonstrate a little ambidextrous skill before being rewarded with a sweet treat. Adding a little adversity between you and the gumball not only makes the toy more interactive and rewarding, but more importantly, cuts down on the number of gumball refills. Now, what type of epic challenge would be worthy of a tasty, colorful orb of endless chewing delight?

## MATERIALS

- ¾" x 5 ½" x 31" (2cm x 14cm x 79cm) pine board for top, bottom, and sides
- ⅛" x 7 ½" x 9 ½" (3mm x 19cm x 24cm) clear acrylic plastic, 2 each
- ½" (13mm) dowel, 11 ¼" (29cm) long, for obstacles and grabbers
- ¼" (6mm) dowel, 12" (30cm) long, 2 each, for handles
- ¾" (2cm) ball, 2 each (optional)
- 8 – 1 ¼" (3cm) coarse-thread drywall screws
- 12 – #4, ⅜" (1cm) pan head screws
- Golf tee
- Gumballs (several thousand pounds, preferably unused)

## TOOLS

- Coping saw
- Miter saw
- Miter box
- Drill with bits: 1" (2.5cm), ⅝" (1.5cm), ⅜" (1cm), ½" (13mm), ¼" (6mm), ⁵⁄₃₂" (40mm), ⅛" (3mm), and counter sink
- Screwdriver

## CHALLENGE 1

I never mastered chopsticks so I think using a chopstick in each hand to lift a gumball out of a box seems like an appropriately high level of difficulty.

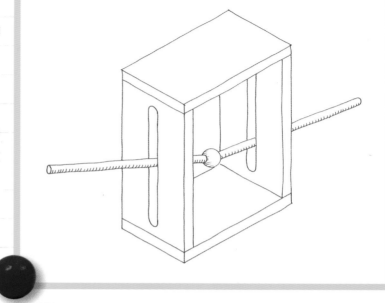

## CHALLENGE 2

As it turns out, lifting a gumball straight up with two chopsticks is rather easy. Let's complicate this by making each chopstick move through a maze.

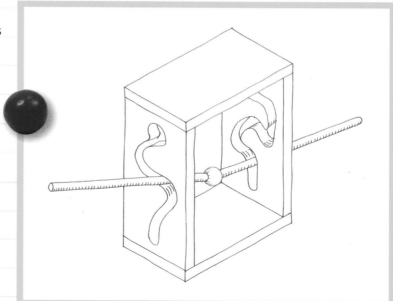

# CHALLENGE 3

Why be nice? Let's add some obstacles inside our box so you really have to work hard to get the gumball and literally taste success.

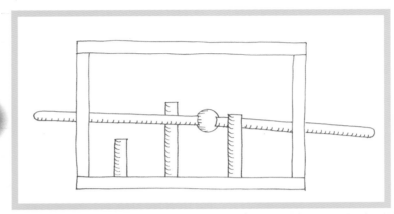

# WIGGLE ROOM

We need a lot of maneuverability for the chopsticks, but the maze tracks can't be too wide or the gumballs will fall out. By beveling the inside and outside edges of the maze we can now move the chopsticks in many directions.

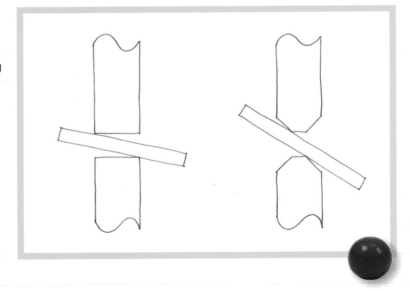

Cut the top, bottom, and sides to size. Make sure the sides are free of knots. For the bottom segment: all holes are drilled ½" (13mm) deep; 5⁄32" (4mm) holes on the side are drilled through and countersunk on the bottom side; the 5⁄32" (4mm) hole in the center is ½" (13mm) deep for the golf tee; the dashed holes are 1" (2.5cm) in diameter and about ⅛" (3mm) deep to capture gumballs; these holes are randomly located.

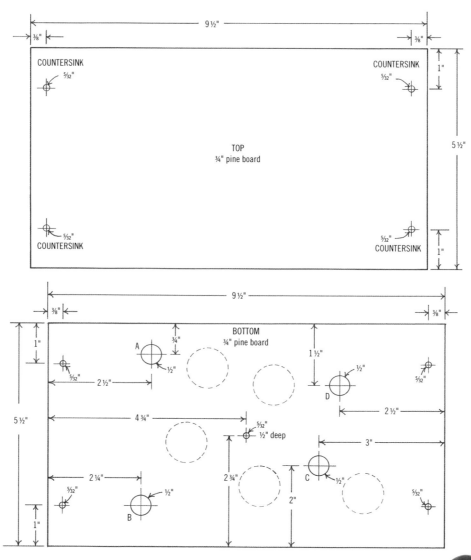

Cut the front and back from clear acrylic.

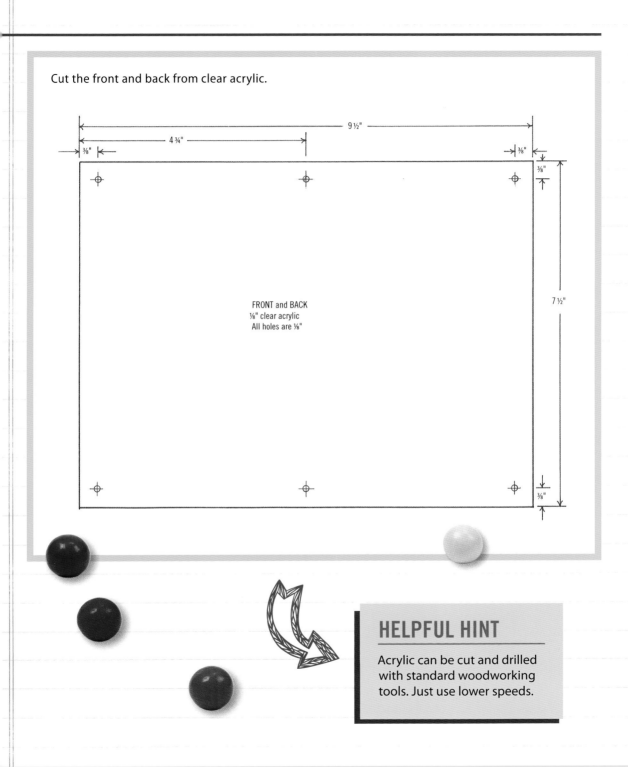

FRONT and BACK
⅛" clear acrylic
All holes are ⅛"

9 ½"
4 ¾"
⅜"
⅜"
⅜"
7 ½"
⅜"

## HELPFUL HINT

Acrylic can be cut and drilled with standard woodworking tools. Just use lower speeds.

Attach the patterns to the sides and bottom (the patterns will be on the inside of the aquarium). Mark the hole locations on the top, front, and back.

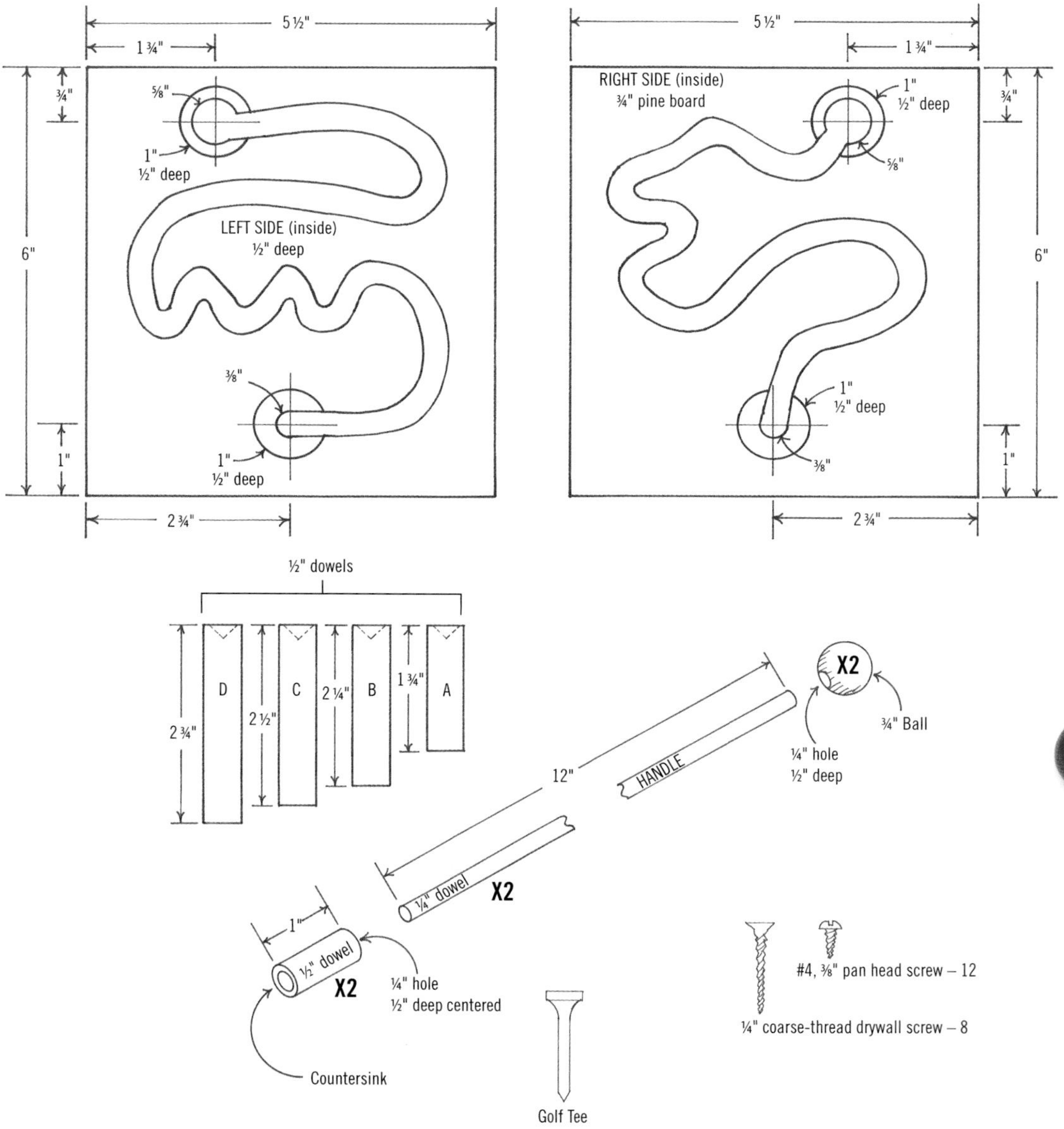

LEFT SIDE (inside)
½" deep

5½"
1¾"
¾"
⅝"
1"
½" deep
6"
⅜"
1"
½" deep
2¾"
1"

RIGHT SIDE (inside)
¾" pine board

5½"
1¾"
¾"
1"
½" deep
⅝"
6"
1"
½" deep
⅜"
2¾"
1"

½" dowels

| D | C | B | A |
|---|---|---|---|

2¾"    2½"    2¼"    1¾"

HANDLE
12"
¼" dowel    X2
¼" hole
½" deep

X2
¾" Ball

1"
½" dowel    X2
¼" hole
½" deep centered

Countersink

Golf Tee

#4, ⅜" pan head screw – 12

¼" coarse-thread drywall screw – 8

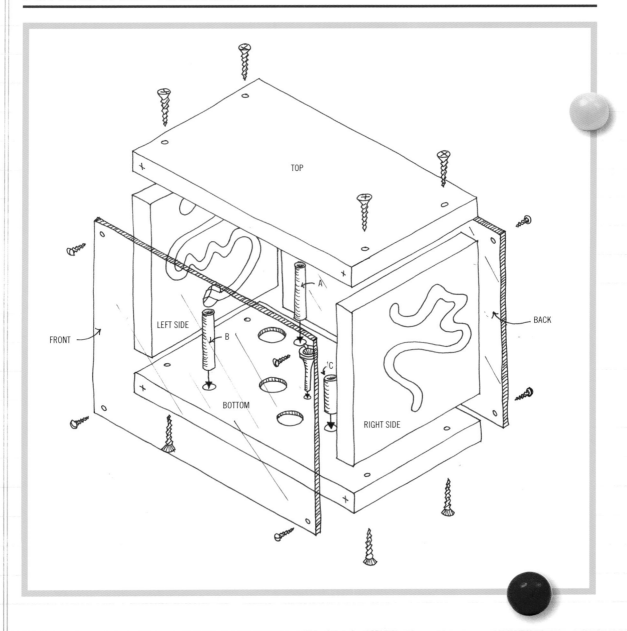

TOP

A

FRONT

LEFT SIDE

B

C

BOTTOM

BACK

RIGHT SIDE

# THE FINISHED PRODUCT

The end result looks a lot like an aquarium, but instead of exotic, shimmering fish, the tank is full of beautiful, multicolored gumballs, all doing their best to escape capture. The seaweed was painted on the outside of the acrylic to make it look more like an aquarium.

**T**hey say, "Necessity is the mother of invention." Well, in this case the only necessity was cleaning my workbench—not my favorite chore. The workbench was littered with a few leftover craft sticks, some oddly shaped wooden scraps, several coins, and lots of sawdust. (Why coins? Because they're perfect for drawing circles and marking corner-rounds.) Anyway, I started to clean up and absentmindedly used a craft stick to flick one of the coins toward the others. The coin flew across the table, ricocheted off a piece of scrap wood, and then smacked into a few of the coins. Hey, that was exciting! I did it a few more times, leaving trails through the sawdust. Soon after that I was sketching and drilling holes trying to concoct a simple machine that keeps this fun going by rapidly launching coin after coin after coin.

## MATERIALS

- ¾" x 2 ½" x 4 ¼"
  (2cm x 6cm x 11cm) pine board
- ⅛" x 2 ½" x 4 ¼"
  (3mm x 6cm x 11cm) plywood
  (Baltic birch works great)
- 4 – craft sticks: ¹⁄₁₆" x ⅜" x
  5" (1.5mm x 1cm x 13cm)
- 7 – #18 X ½" (13mm) wire nails
- 10–15 – ¹⁄₁₆" (1.5mm) thick,
  ¹¹⁄₁₆" (17mm) diameter metal
  disks (dimes, that is!)

## TOOLS

- Drill with bits:
  ¹⁄₁₆" (1.5mm), ¾" (2cm)
- Scroll saw
- Hammer
- Ruler
- Square
- Pencil
- Scissors
- Sandpaper
- Glue

## WHICH COIN TO LAUNCH?

If you want to hold a bunch of coins, then choose the smallest—the dime. Fortunately, they are also slightly thinner than a craft stick so making a track for them is easy.

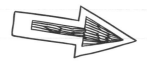

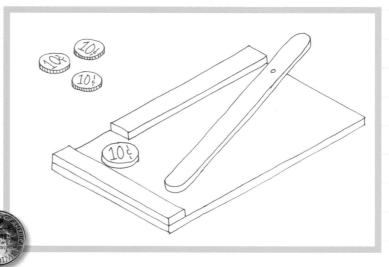

## FLICKING COINS

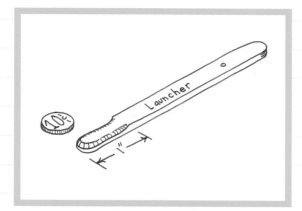

A craft stick worked great on the workbench. If a nail is used as a pivot, the dime can be hit very hard. Other craft sticks will guide the dime and stop the striker.

## HOLDING LOTS OF DIMES

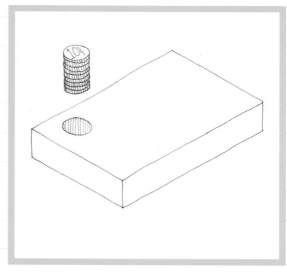

To make this rapid-fire, there needs to be a stack of dimes over the launch area. A ¾" (2cm) hole in a ¾" (2cm) thick board will hold about 10 dimes. That should be plenty. We will mount this above what we've already made.

# MINOR MALFUNCTION

Once in a while the striker would get stuck and fail to launch a dime. After some troubleshooting I discovered the problem—the striker kept hitting the dime above. This jamming problem was easily fixed by sanding the leading edge of the striker so it smoothly passes under the dime above.

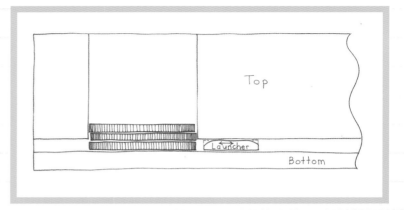

# CREATING THE PARTS

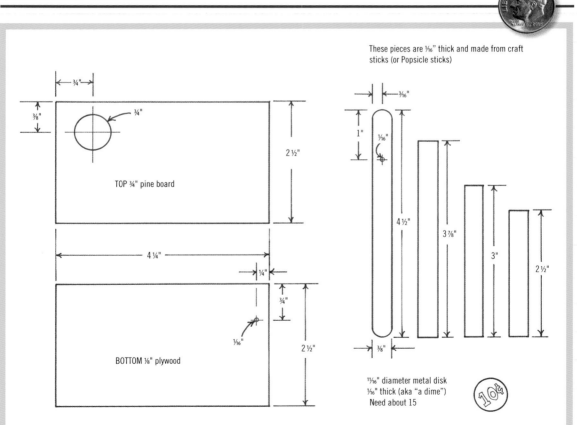

¾"

⅜"

¾"

2½"

TOP ¾" pine board

4¼"

¼"

¾"

1/16"

2½"

BOTTOM ⅛" plywood

These pieces are 1/16" thick and made from craft sticks (or Popsicle sticks)

3/16"

1"

1/16"

4½"

⅜"

3⅞"

3"

2½"

11/16" diameter metal disk
1/16" thick (aka "a dime")
Need about 15

10¢

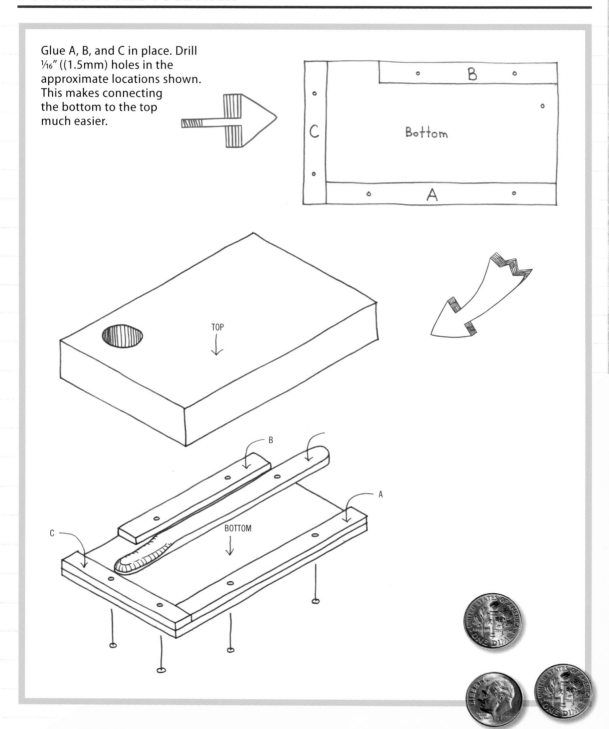

Glue A, B, and C in place. Drill ¹⁄₁₆" ((1.5mm) holes in the approximate locations shown. This makes connecting the bottom to the top much easier.

B

C

Bottom

A

TOP

B

A

C

BOTTOM

# POCKET GUMBALL LAUNCHER

Sure you can carry gumballs in your pocket, but do you or your friends really want to pop a sticky, lint-covered ball of chewy sweetness into your mouth? I didn't think so. You could put them in a bag or a box, but that's too boring. What we really want is a pocket-sized gadget that dispenses one gumball at a time to any of our nearby friends—basically a gumball air delivery system. Here are the requirements:

1. Fits in a pocket.

2. Dispenses one gumball at a time, but holds many.

3. Can deliver a gumball up to 10 feet away.

## MATERIALS

- ¾" x ¾" x 7" (2cm x 2cm x 18cm) pine board
- ¼" x ¾" x 17" (6mm x 2cm x 18cm) pine board
- ⅛" x 3" x 10" (3mm x 7.5cm x 25cm) plywood for front and back
- 2 – 1" (2.5cm) pegs cut to ½" (13mm) length
- 2 – ½" (13mm) brad round head
- 1 - #32, 3" x ⅛" (7.5cm x 3mm) rubber band
- Alternative: ⅛" x 3" x 5" (3mm x 7.5cm x 13cm) acrylic for front
- Gumballs (as many as you can!)
- Wood glue or epoxy if front is made from acrylic

## TOOLS

- Drill with bits: ¹⁄₁₆" (1.5mm), ⁷⁄₃₂" (5mm)
- Scroll saw
- Miter saw
- Hammer
- Tape measure
- Square
- Pencil
- Scissors
- Sandpaper
- Thin wire (for threading rubber band)

## SIZE

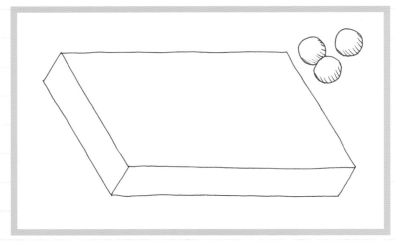

Obviously this contraption should be slightly smaller than a pocket—about 3" (7.5cm) by 5" (13cm). Gumballs are about ⅝" (1.5cm) diameter so a 1" (2.5cm) thick box will hold quite a few.

## DISPENSE

This is the tricky part—one and only one gumball can be loaded and launched at a time. The gumball needs to be loaded when the ramrod is pulled back. A small ramp that holds only one gumball will do the trick. Tilting our gumball machine down and back up will put one gumball on the ramp.

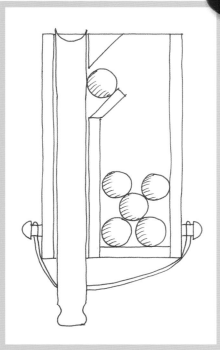

## LAUNCH

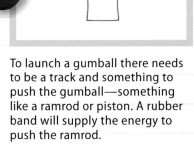

To launch a gumball there needs to be a track and something to push the gumball—something like a ramrod or piston. A rubber band will supply the energy to push the ramrod.

## SOMETHING'S WRONG

The rubber band breaks after about 5 launches. The upward motion of the ramrod is stopped by the rubber band hitting the bottom. This acts like a scissors and shears off the rubber band. The solution is to thin the handle to give the rubber band room to move and round all the corners. Now we can deliver gumballs all day long.

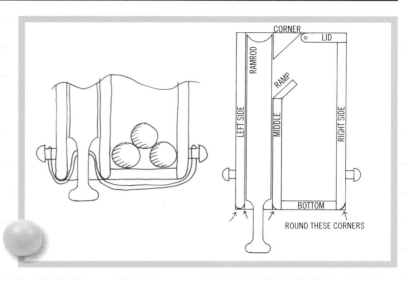

## CREATING THE PARTS

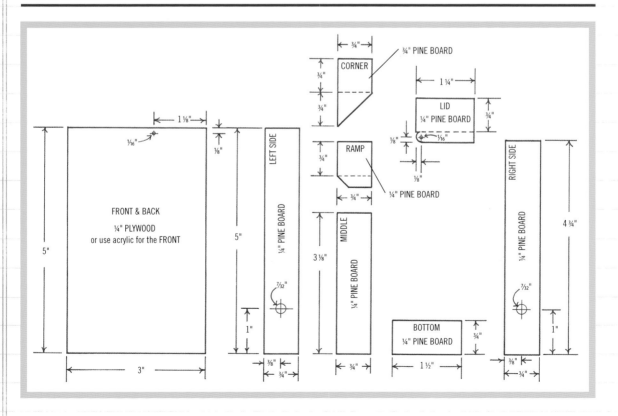

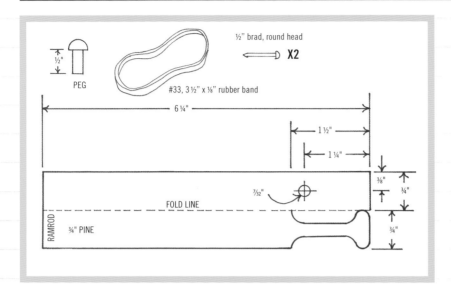

½" brad, round head

⟸▭▷ **X2**

PEG

#33, 3 ½" x ⅛" rubber band

6 ¼"

1 ½"

1 ¼"

³⁄₈"

¾"

⁷⁄₃₂"

FOLD LINE

RAMROD

¾" PINE

¾"

# PUTTING IT ALL TOGETHER

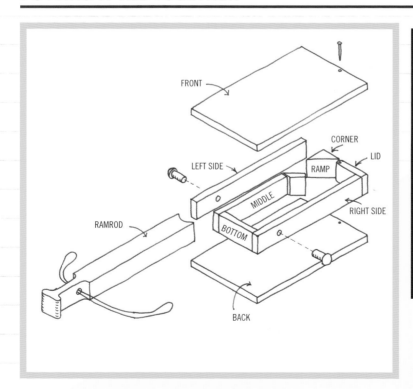

FRONT

CORNER

LID

LEFT SIDE

RAMP

MIDDLE

RIGHT SIDE

RAMROD

BOTTOM

BACK

## HELPFUL HINT

Pegs can be purchased in most hobby stores or online. The shaft is typically about 1" long and ¹⁵⁄₆₄" wide. This allows them to fit snugly in a ⁷⁄₃₂" hole without falling out. Or they can be used as an axle for a wheel that has a ¼" hole. Store-bought pegs should be on every inventor's workbench.

# PING-PONG® BALL EXPLOSION

## MATERIALS

- ¾" x 7" x 10"
  (2cm x 18cm x 25cm)
  pin board—base
- ¾" x 2" x 6" (2cm x 5cm x 15cm)
  pine board—2 supports
- ¾" x 2" x 2" (2cm x 5cm x 5cm)
  pine board—latch
- ¾" x 3" x 3" (2cm x 7.5cm x 7.5cm)
  pine board—top
- ½" x 2" x 3" (13mm x 5cm x 7.5cm)
  plywood—paddle
- 4 – ½" (13mm) dowel
  18" (46cm) long
- ⅜" (1cm) dowel 10" (25cm) long—
  axle and arm
- 2 – 1" x ¼" (2.5cm x 6mm) pegs
- 1 ½" (4cm) diameter wooden ball
- 4 – 1 ½" (4cm) coarse-thread
  drywall screws
- #112 x 1⅜" (3.5cm) L-hook (aka
  square bend hook)
- #208 or #210 screw eye
- 10 – Ping-Pong® balls
- 1 rubber band 7" (18cm) x ⅛" (3mm)
  such as the Brites® File Bands, or 3
  #64 (3½" x ¼", 9cm x 6mm) rubber
  bands looped together

## TOOLS

- Miter saw
- Scroll saw
- Drill with bits:
  ¹⁄₁₆" (1.5mm), ⅛" (3mm),
  ⁵⁄₃₂" (4mm), ⁷⁄₃₂" (5mm),
  ¼" (6mm), ⁷⁄₁₆" (11mm),
  ⅜" (1cm), ½" (13mm),
  counter sink
- Phillips screwdriver
- Hammer
- Ruler
- Compass
- Square
- Protractor, or 30-60-90
  triangle, pencil
- Sandpaper
- Scissors

**W**hat started off as an afternoon ping-pong game became the catalyst for this toy creation. After a few ferocious and dizzying games of run-around-ping-pong (obviously, we're not serious Ping-Pong players), I was idly bouncing a ball on the paddle. That's when it happened. For reasons unknown, something deep inside my brain impulsively yelled, "Smash it!" So, I hit the ball as hard as possible and excitedly watched it sail up and away through the air. There was no chance of a second hit so my thoughts drifted to building a mechanism that could hit Ping-Pong balls straight up with more accuracy. The result was this contraption. It blasts a Ping-Pong ball high into the sky. While testing it out, for reasons unknown, something deep inside my brain mischievously yelled, "Put in lots of Ping-Pong balls," and that's when I experienced the fun of Ping-Pong Ball Explosion.

## ACCURACY

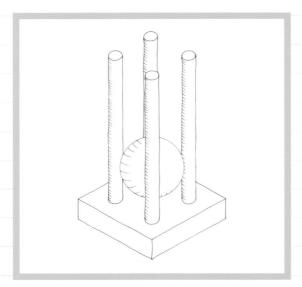

We want our Ping-Pong ball to blast straight up. The easiest way to do this is to make a long track for the ball to follow.

## LATCH

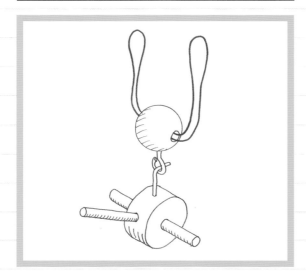

We'll want to latch the wooden sphere in the down position while we aim our contraption straight up.

## LAUNCH POWER

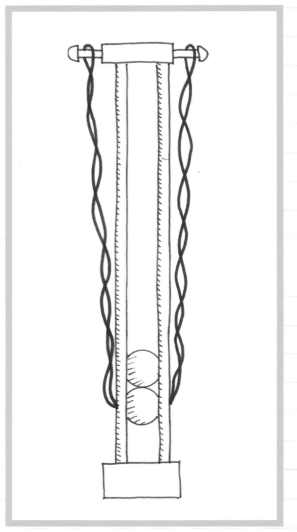

Instead of hitting the ball, we'll push it up the track. A large rubber band connected to a wooden sphere will do the pushing. The rubber band gives us plenty of acceleration, and the sphere won't get jammed in the track.

## ADDING SOME FUN

By adding a target to the handle on the latch, we can launch our ball with a beanbag. This adds an element of surprise. And if we put in a whole bunch of balls, we'll have a Ping-Pong ball explosion!

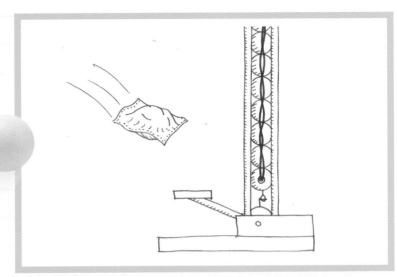

## CREATING THE PARTS

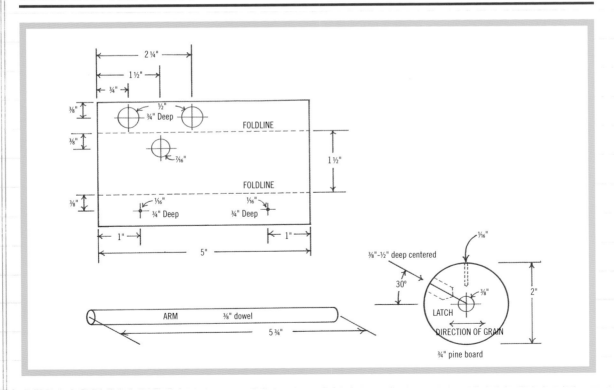

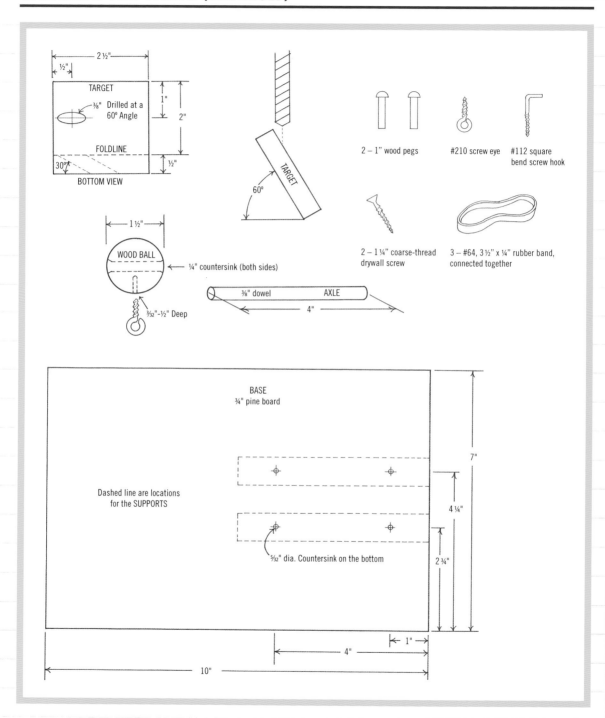

2½"

½"

TARGET

⅜" Drilled at a 60° Angle

1"

2"

FOLDLINE

30°

½"

BOTTOM VIEW

TARGET

60°

2 – 1" wood pegs

#210 screw eye

#112 square bend screw hook

1½"

WOOD BALL

¼" countersink (both sides)

³⁄₃₂"–½" Deep

2 – 1¼" coarse-thread drywall screw

3 – #64, 3½" x ¼" rubber band, connected together

⅜" dowel   AXLE

4"

BASE
¾" pine board

7"

4¼"

Dashed line are locations for the SUPPORTS

2¾"

⁵⁄₃₂" dia. Countersink on the bottom

1"

4"

10"

# PUTTING IT ALL TOGETHER

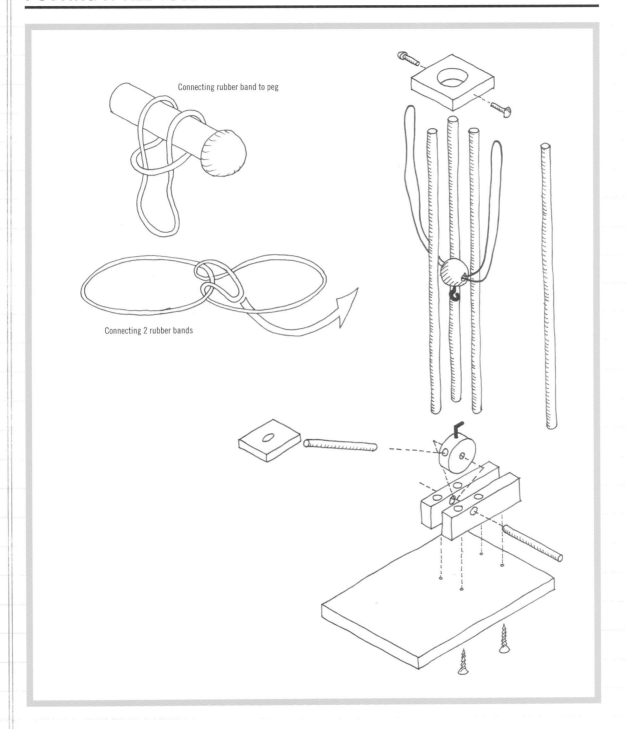

Connecting rubber band to peg

Connecting 2 rubber bands

# PAY DIRT GUMBALL MAZE

**W**ouldn't it be fun to build a game that rewards you more and more as you get better and better? Ever play with one of those toys where you have to roll a tiny ball through a maze? The first time is almost impossible and takes forever. But as you practice, you get faster and faster. Unfortunately, whether you're a beginner or a professional maze ball-roller, the reward is the same—you pat yourself on the back and say, "Well done, Self!" Personally, I'd like to get some type of reward, like more and more candy, as my skill improves over time. When that expert level is finally achieved after hours and hours of hard work, I want to hit pay dirt—candy galore! Let's make a toy that does just that. We'll use a maze and tasty round gumballs instead a tiny metal ball.

## MATERIALS

- ¾" x 1 ¾" x 40"
  (2cm x 4.5cm x 102cm) pine board
- 1" x 1" x 3 ¾"
  (2.5cm x 2.5cm x 9.5cm)
  pine board
- ¼" x ¾" x 20"
  (6mm x 2cm x 51cm) pine board
- ¼" x 8 ½" x 8 ½"
  (6mm x 22cm x 22cm)
  plywood board or Masonite
- ¼" x 7" x 7"
  (6mm x 18cm x 18cm)
  plywood board or Masonite
- ⅛" x 8 ½" x 8 ½"
  (3mm x 22cm x 22cm) acrylic plastic
- 8 – 1 ½" (4cm) coarse-thread
  drywall screws
- 4 – #4⅜" (1cm) pan head
  Phillips screws
- Glue

## TOOLS

- Drill with bits:
  ¹⁄₁₆" (1.5mm), ⅛" (3mm), ⁵⁄₃₂"
  (4mm), ³⁄₁₆" (4.5mm), ¾" (2cm)
- Phillips screwdriver
- Standard screwdriver
- Table saw
- Scroll saw
- Miter saw
- Tape measure
- Square
- Awl
- Pencil
- Scissors
- Permanent marker (for
  marking on plastic)
- Sandpaper

## THE MAZE

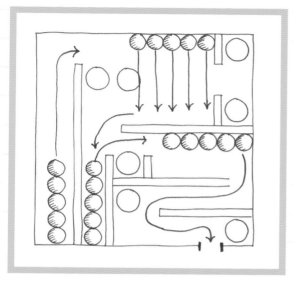

Usually a maze is designed for one ball at a time. For our game, five gumballs will be moved through the maze, so if you are very skilled you will get an entire handful of sweet treats. If you are lacking in skill, you will get none, zero, zilch. Don't be disheartened; you did win a chance to practice some more.

## LOADING

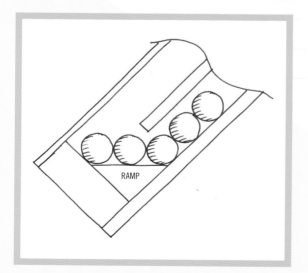

## THE CHALLENGE

There will be holes in the floor of the maze to snatch your gumballs if you're careless.

## HOW THICK

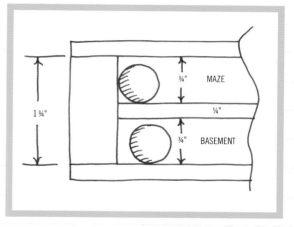

The tracks for the gumballs need to be ¾" (2cm) x ¾" (2cm). If we want the gumballs to fall through the floor, then there needs to be a basement that is ¾" (2cm) deep. The math says the sides need to be 1 ¾" (4.5cm) wide—and math doesn't lie.

The round candy delights will be stored in the basement of the maze. A ramp will bring them to the top level by tilting the maze. The gumballs will roll through a slot rather than a hole, so 5 to 6 gumballs can be loaded at the same time.

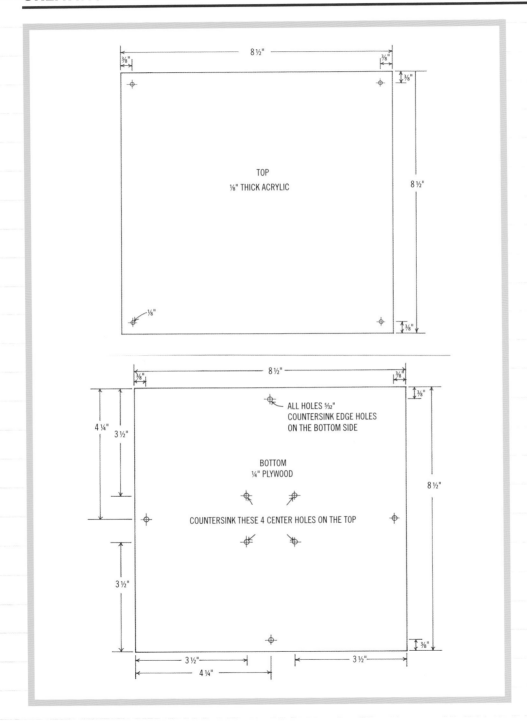

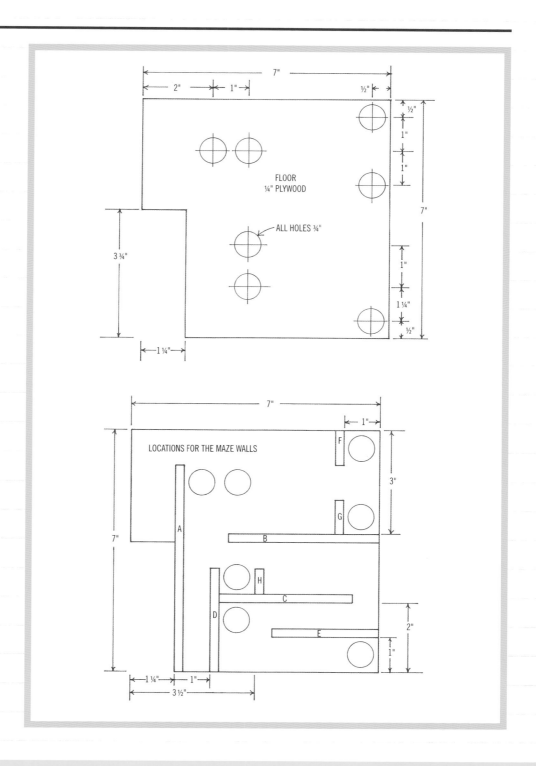

FLOOR
¼" PLYWOOD

ALL HOLES ¾"

LOCATIONS FOR THE MAZE WALLS

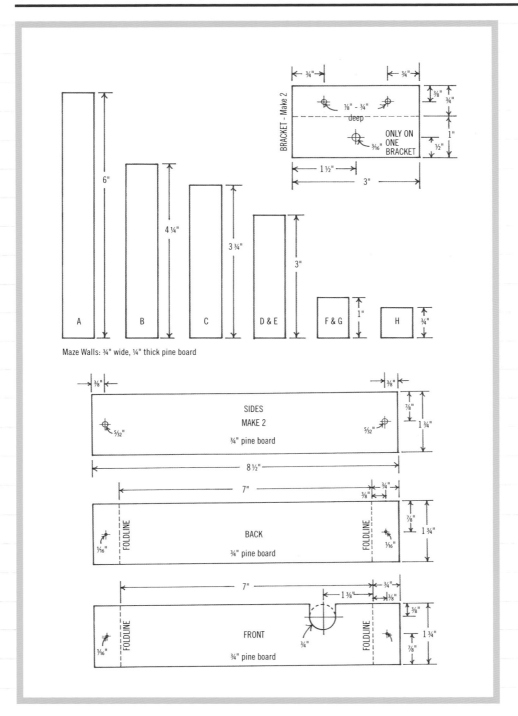

BRACKET - Make 2

¾" ¾"

⅜" ¾"

⅛" – ¾" deep

ONLY ON ONE BRACKET

3/16"

1"

½"

1½"

3"

6"

4¼"

3¾"

3"

1"

¾"

A    B    C    D & E    F & G    H

Maze Walls: ¾" wide, ¼" thick pine board

⅜"    ⅜"

SIDES
MAKE 2
¾" pine board

⅞"

1¾"

5/32"    5/32"

8½"

7"    ¾"
⅜"

BACK
¾" pine board

⅞"

1¾"

1/16"    FOLDLINE    FOLDLINE    1/16"

7"    ¾"
1⅜"    ⅜"

⅜"

FRONT
¾" pine board

¾"

⅞"

1¾"

1/16"    FOLDLINE    FOLDLINE

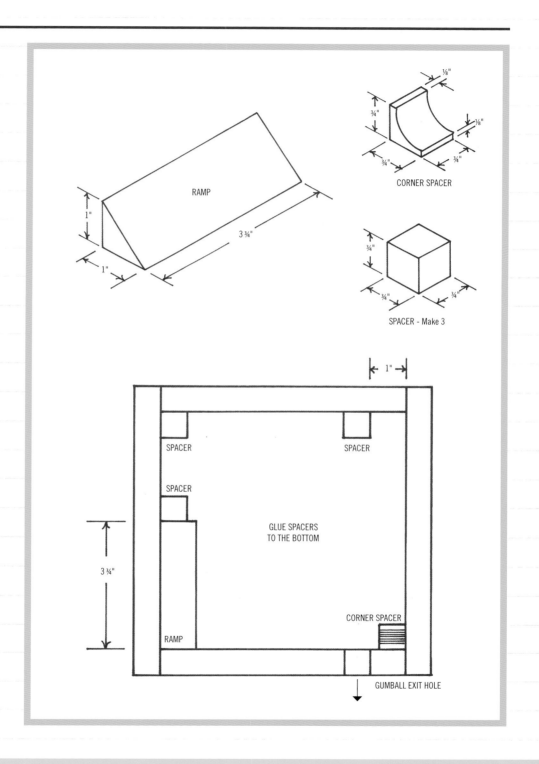

RAMP

1"

1"

3 ¾"

CORNER SPACER

⅛"

¾"

¾"

¾"

⅛"

SPACER - Make 3

¾"

¾"

¾"

1"

SPACER

SPACER

SPACER

GLUE SPACERS
TO THE BOTTOM

3 ¾"

RAMP

CORNER SPACER

GUMBALL EXIT HOLE

# PUTTING IT ALL TOGETHER

## HELPFUL HINT

Connect front, back, and sides, then mount onto the Bottom. Glue the Spacers and Ramp in place. Check that the Floor fits inside before gluing the Maze pieces in place.

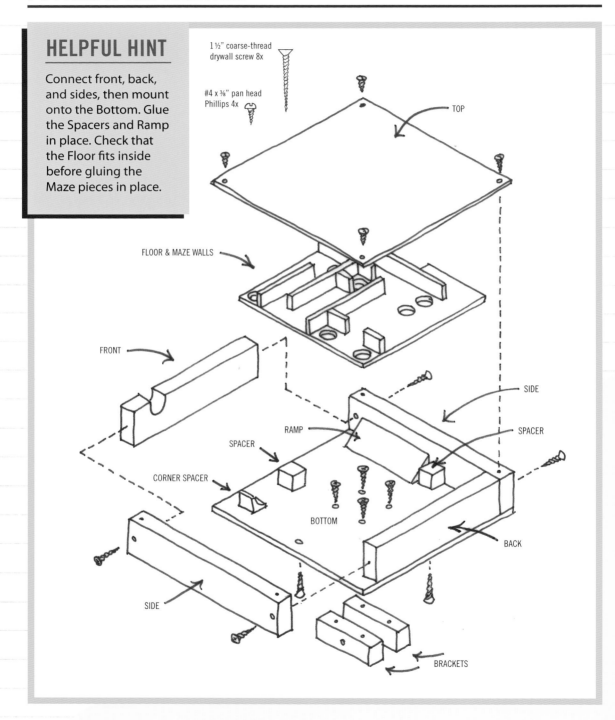

1 ½" coarse-thread drywall screw 8x

#4 x ⅜" pan head Phillips 4x

TOP

FLOOR & MAZE WALLS

FRONT

SIDE

SPACER

RAMP

SPACER

CORNER SPACER

BOTTOM

SIDE

BACK

BRACKETS

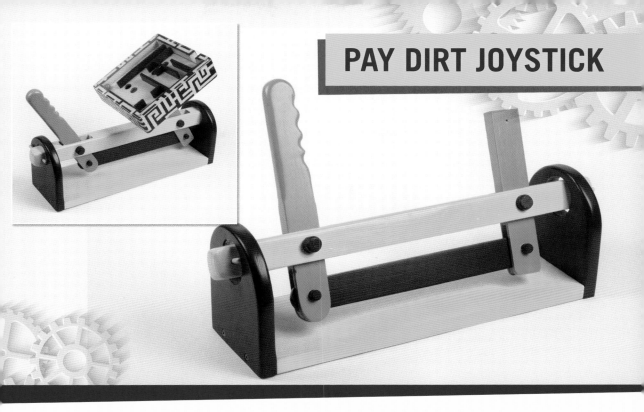

**I**f you've mastered the Pay Dirt Gumball Maze, then you are enjoying a handful of gum whenever you want it. Now it's time to add yet another challenge. The required movement of the maze reminds me of the pitch and roll of an airplane. In smaller planes this is sometimes controlled by a joystick. Adding a joystick to the maze will definitely add a new challenge. The joystick also adds an eye-catching mechanism to attract the curious minds that will appreciate your craftsmanship.

## SKILL LEVELS

**NEWBY**—Sorry, no gumball. As they say, "Practice, Practice, Practice!"
**TRAINEE**—1 gumball. I like where you're going. Keep working hard.
**PAY DIRT**—A handful of gumballs. You've got talent! You're unstoppable!

## MATERIALS

- ¾" x 5 ½" x 28"
  (2cm x 14cm x 71cm)
  pine board
- ¾" x 1 ½" x 19"
  (2cm x 4cm x 48cm) pine board
- 1 ½" x 1 ½" x 19 ⅝"
  (4cm x 4cm x 50cm) pine board
- ¼" x 1 ½" x 13"
  (6mm x 4cm x 33cm) pine board
- ¾" (2cm) dowel, 4½" (11cm) long
- ½" (13mm) dowel, 3" (7.5cm) long
- ¼" (6mm) dowel, 5 ½" (14cm) long
- 1 – 2" (5cm) coarse-thread drywall screw
- 4 – 1 ½" (4cm) coarse-thread drywall screws

## TOOLS

- Drill with bits: ⅛" (3 mm), 5⁄32" (4mm), ¼" (6mm), ½" (13mm), ¾" (2cm), counter sink, 2" (5cm) hole cutter
- Phillips screwdriver
- Scroll saw
- Miter saw
- Tape measure
- Square
- Awl
- Pencil
- Scissors
- Compass
- Sandpaper

PAY DIRT JOYSTICK **47**

## SIMPLE JOYSTICK

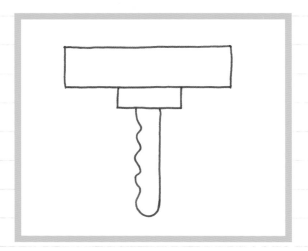

We can just put a handle on the bottom of the maze—too boring!

## PITCH *(FORWARD AND BACKWARD TILT)*

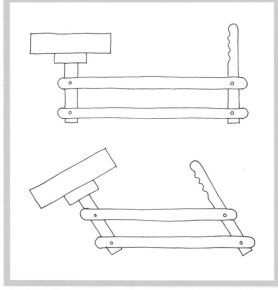

An easy way to get pitch is to use a parallelogram.

## ROLL *(LEFT AND RIGHT TILT)*

This is accomplished by rigidly mounting the joystick and maze to a dowel supported by end pieces.

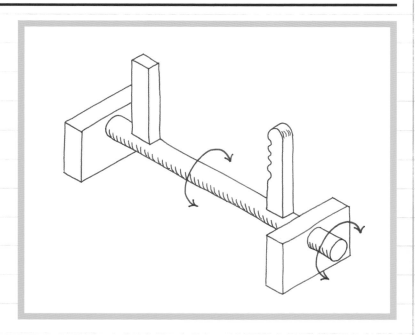

# PITCH AND ROLL

Combining the two is a bit more complicated. We constructed the parallelogram to control pitch with square boards because they are easy to cut. For roll we use a round hole to allow for rotation. You've probably heard the expression "you can't put a square peg in a round hole." Well, to make this contraption we will toss out conventional wisdom and put our square board in a round hole.

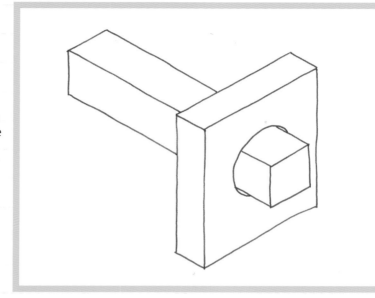

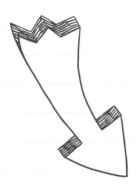

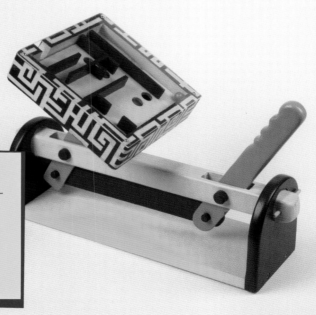

## DECORATION

Try adding an "honesty" box on the side to help pay for more gumballs. A simple box with a coin slot and a suggestion of "5¢ per try" might just fund your next invention.

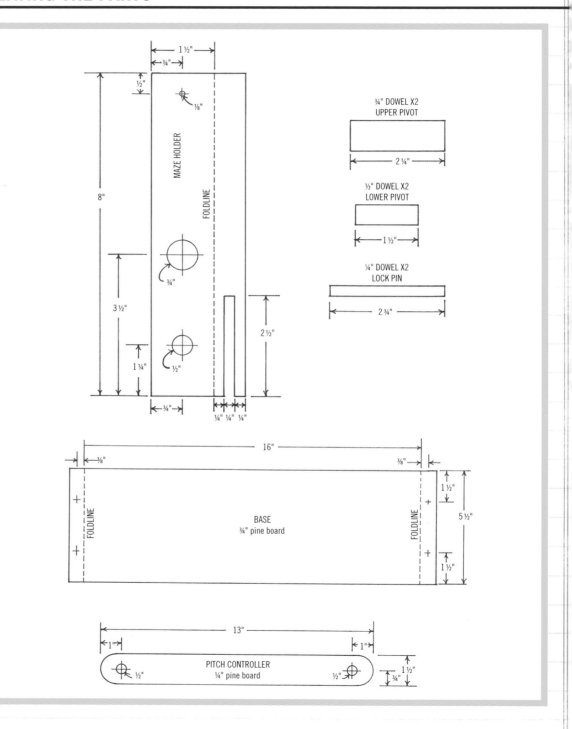

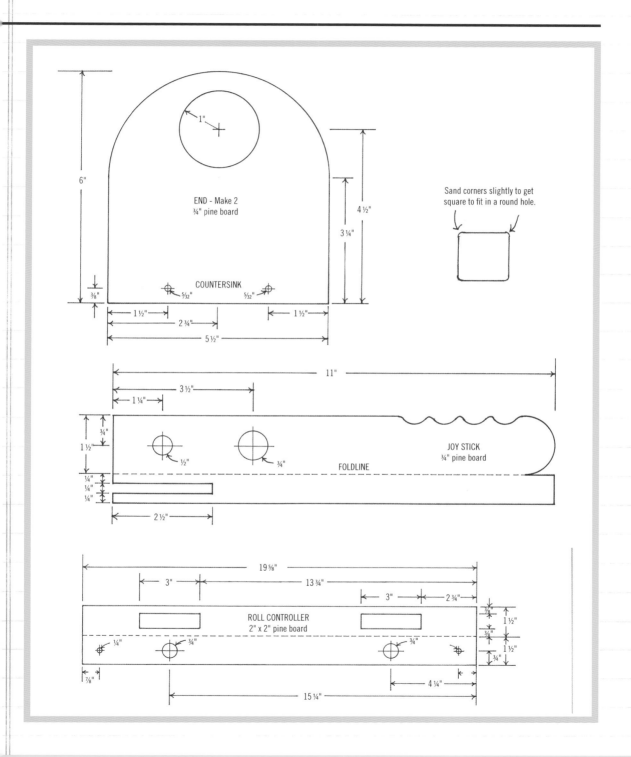

6"

END - Make 2
¾" pine board

1"

4 ½"

3 ¼"

⅜"

COUNTERSINK

5/32"    5/32"

1 ½"

2 ¾"

1 ½"

5 ½"

Sand corners slightly to get
square to fit in a round hole.

11"

3 ½"

1 ¼"

¾"

1 ½"

½"

¾"

FOLDLINE

JOY STICK
¾" pine board

¼"
¼"
¼"

2 ½"

19 ⅝"

3"

13 ¾"

3"

2 ¾"

⅜"

1 ½"

ROLL CONTROLLER
2" x 2" pine board

⅜"

1 ½"

¼"

¾"

¾"

¾"

⅞"

4 ¼"

15 ¼"

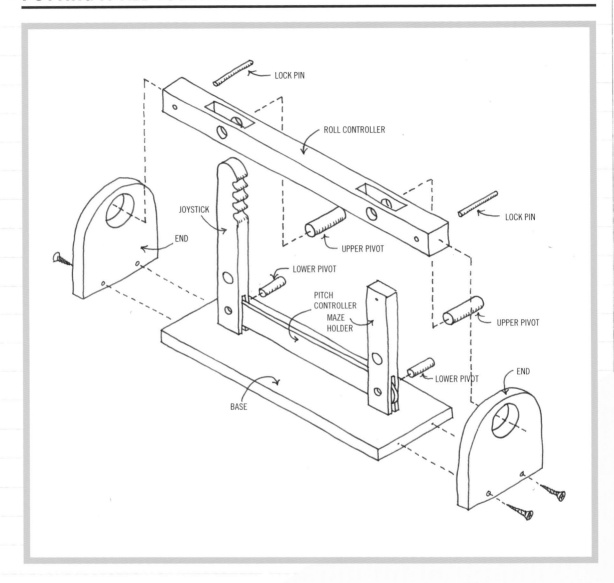

LOCK PIN

ROLL CONTROLLER

LOCK PIN

JOYSTICK

END

UPPER PIVOT

LOWER PIVOT

PITCH
CONTROLLER
MAZE
HOLDER

UPPER PIVOT

LOWER PIVOT

END

BASE

# TORNADO BOX

**H**ow would you like to own a special box so strong and impenetrable that only the overwhelming power of a tornado can open it? Keep your prized possessions safe by locking them inside. Hand the box to a friend, and they won't be able to open it. But you, and the tornado, know the secret. Spin the box with either your hands or a mighty wind. A secret mechanism releases the lid and allows it to be lifted off with no effort.

## MATERIALS

- ¾" x 5 ¼" x 31"
  (2cm x 13cm x 79cm)
  pine board
- ¼" x 3 ¾" x 3 ¾"
  (6mm x 9.5cm x 9.5cm)
  plywood board
- ¼" (6mm) steel rod,
  5" (13cm) long
- ⅜" (1cm) dowel, 3" (7.5cm) long
- 13 – 1 ½" (4cm) coarse-thread
  drywall screws

## TOOLS

- Drill with bits:
  1/16" (1.5mm), 5/32" (4mm),
  9/32" (28mm), ⅜" (1cm)
- Phillips screwdriver
- Table saw
- Miter saw
- Scroll saw
- Hacksaw
- Tape measure
- Square
- Awl
- Pencil
- Scissors
- Sandpaper
- Metal file

## CENTRIPETAL FORCE

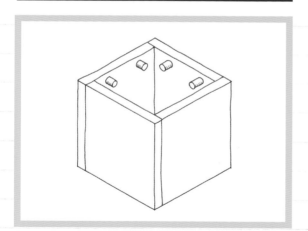

We want to unlock our box with a spinning motion, so imagine being on a merry-go-round that's going faster and faster. If you are at the edge you will have to hang on tighter and tighter to keep from being thrown off the side. We will spin our box horizontally to create the same force that wants to toss you off the merry-go-round

## THE PROBLEM

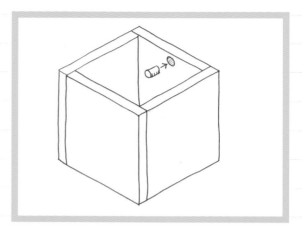

With only a single pin, a thief can get lucky by tilting the box in one direction and release the lid. This problem is eliminated by putting two pins on each side so that no matter how the box is tilted, some pins will still be engaged with the lid.

## SIMPLE LOCK

A metal pin in the side of our box can lock it. Spinning the box would force the pin into the hole and release the lid.

## THE LID

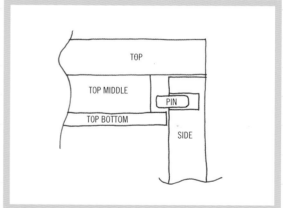

The pins must engage the lid if it is to stay locked. Here's one way to do it that doesn't require much precision.

## CREATING THE PARTS

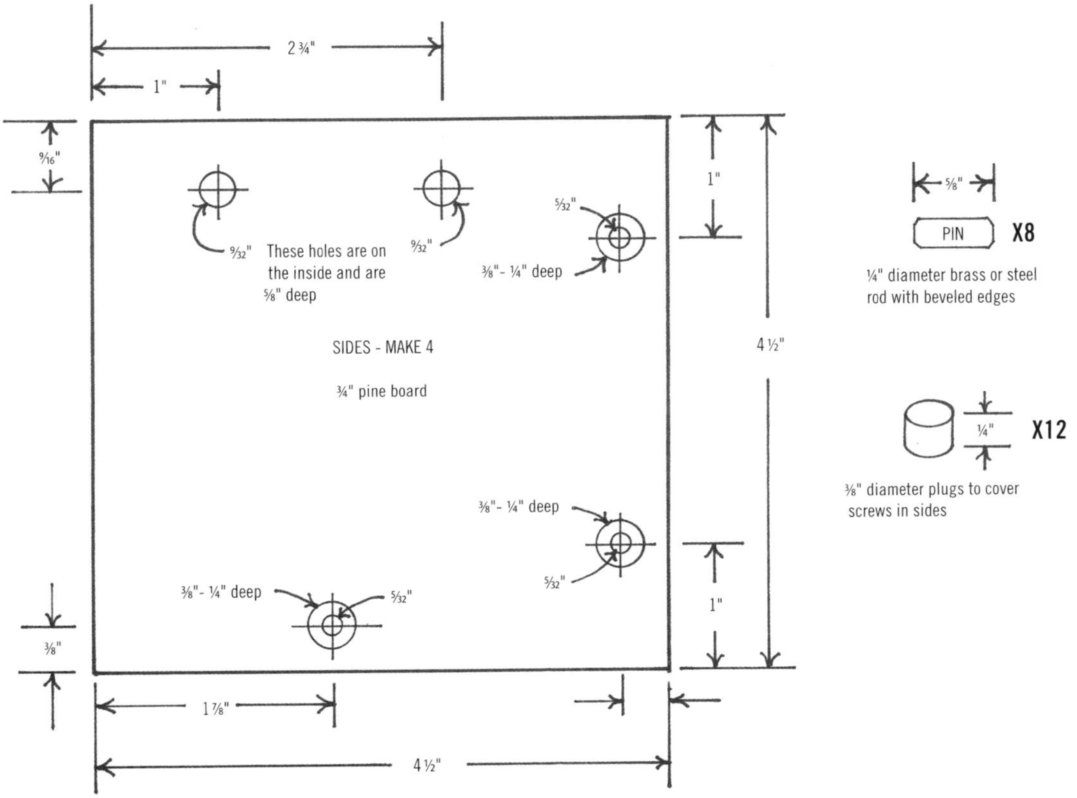

2 3/4"
1"
9/16"
9/32"
These holes are on the inside and are 5/8" deep
9/32"
5/32"
3/8"- 1/4" deep
1"
SIDES - MAKE 4
3/4" pine board
4 1/2"
3/8"- 1/4" deep
5/32"
3/8"- 1/4" deep
5/32"
1"
3/8"
1 7/8"
4 1/2"
5/8"
PIN
X8
1/4" diameter brass or steel rod with beveled edges
1/4"
X12
3/8" diameter plugs to cover screws in sides


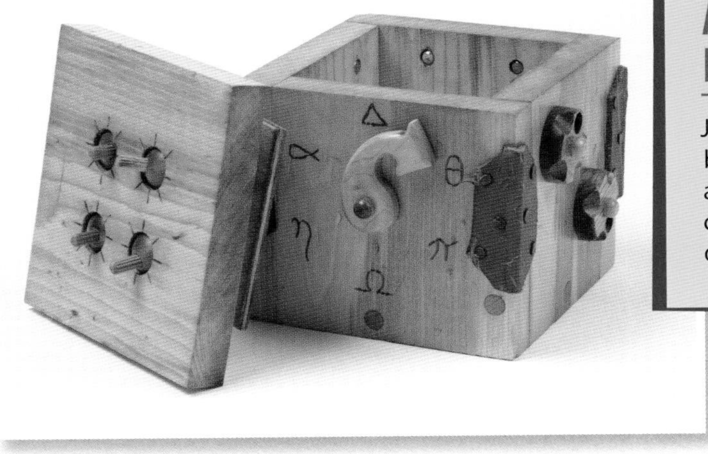

### ADD SOME FRUSTRATION

Just for grins I decorated the box by adding some arrows, knobs, and joysticks to look like secret combination locks. This will really discourage a potential thief.

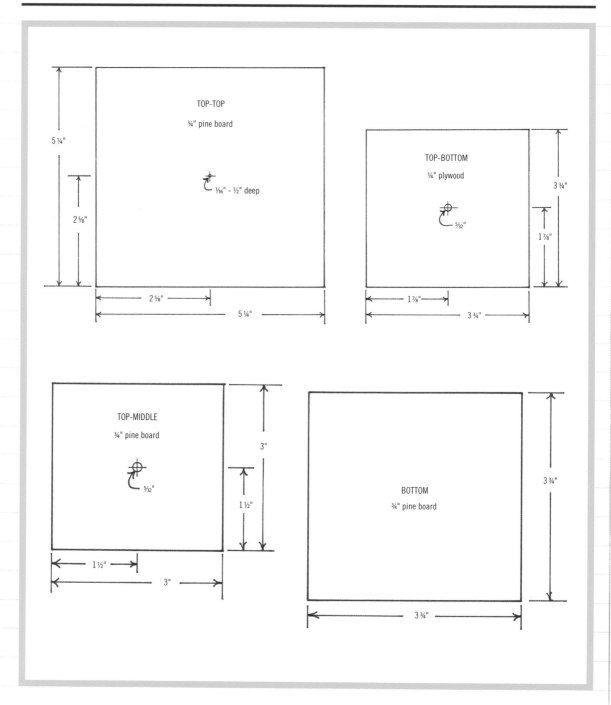

TOP-TOP

¾" pine board

¹⁄₁₆" - ½" deep

5 ¼"

2 ⅝"

2 ⅝"

5 ¼"

TOP-BOTTOM

¼" plywood

⁵⁄₃₂"

3 ¾"

1 ⅞"

1 ⅞"

3 ¾"

TOP-MIDDLE

¾" pine board

⁵⁄₃₂"

3"

1 ½"

1 ½"

3"

BOTTOM

¾" pine board

3 ¾"

3 ¾"

# PUTTING IT ALL TOGETHER

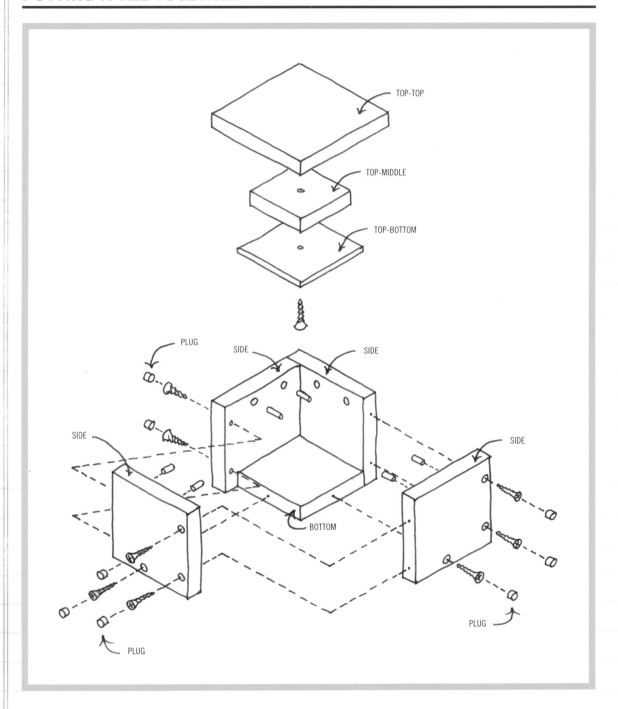

TOP-TOP

TOP-MIDDLE

TOP-BOTTOM

PLUG

SIDE

SIDE

SIDE

SIDE

BOTTOM

PLUG

PLUG

# BIRD POOP SPLATTER-ER

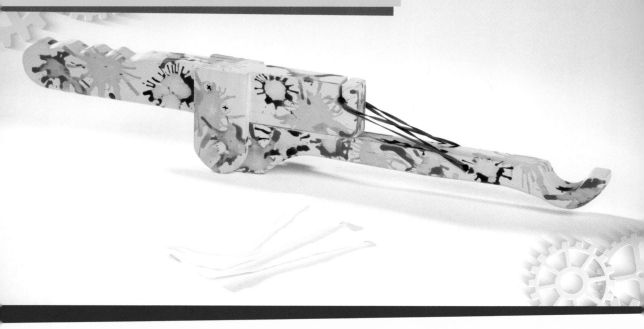

This toy sounds like it was created after a sneak attack from a bird and my desire to get even with the little flying fellow. But really my inspiration was to throw a ball of water a long distance with great accuracy. Not a squirt of water, mind you; that's called a squirt gun. I'm talking about hurling just a small volume of water—like a small snowball, only melted. My first thought was something like a miniature water balloon. There are two main problems with water balloons: (1) you have to be able to fill them, and (2) you have to have balloons, duh! This toy eliminates both of these obstacles by using a simple tissue to hold and deliver the water. The soaked tissue delivers a loud, wet "splat" sound and marks the target with that distinctive "splatter" pattern usually created by our flying friends—hence the name.

## MATERIALS

- ¾" x 1 ½" x 21" (2cm x 4cm x 53cm) pine board
- ¼" x 1 ½" x 6" (6mm x 4cm x 15cm) plywood board
- ⅜" (1cm) dowel, 1 ¾" (4.5cm) long
- 4 – 1" (2.5cm) coarse-thread drywall screws
- 1 – #64, 3 ½" x ¼" (9cm x 6mm) rubber band
- Tissues (nose-blowing size)
- Water

## TOOLS

- Drill with bits: ¹⁄₁₆" (1.5mm), ⁵⁄₃₂" (4mm), ¼" (6mm), ⅜" (1cm), ¹³⁄₃₂" (1cm)
- Phillips screwdriver
- Scroll saws
- Tape measure
- Square
- Awl
- Pencil
- Scissors
- Compass
- Sandpaper

## WATER DELIVER

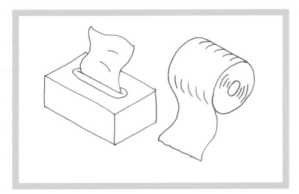

My first attempts to shoot just a ball of water all pretty much failed with just a spray of water dispersed randomly around the shop. Abandoning that train of thought, I decided that something should carry the water. Some ideas included a water balloon, sponge, or tissue. The tissue sounded perfect because it was absorbent, cheap, and easy to get.

## TOSSING A TISSUE

Making the cup at the end of a stick will help fling our wet tissue plenty far and with great accuracy. Is this an original idea? Nope, it's basically a lacrosse stick.

## HOLDING A WET TISSUE

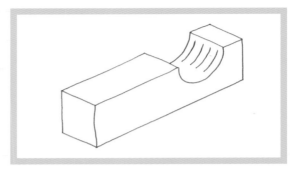

Wet tissues are obviously not very strong. They need to be supported in a cup for launching.

## STICKING TISSUES

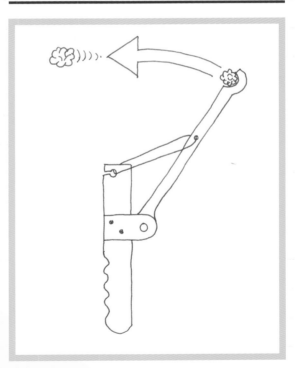

Once in a while the tissue would stick in the cup a little, thus changing the flight pattern—that is, I couldn't hit a darn thing. A spring-loaded hinge was added to the middle of the stick to create a sudden stop to dislodge the tissue.

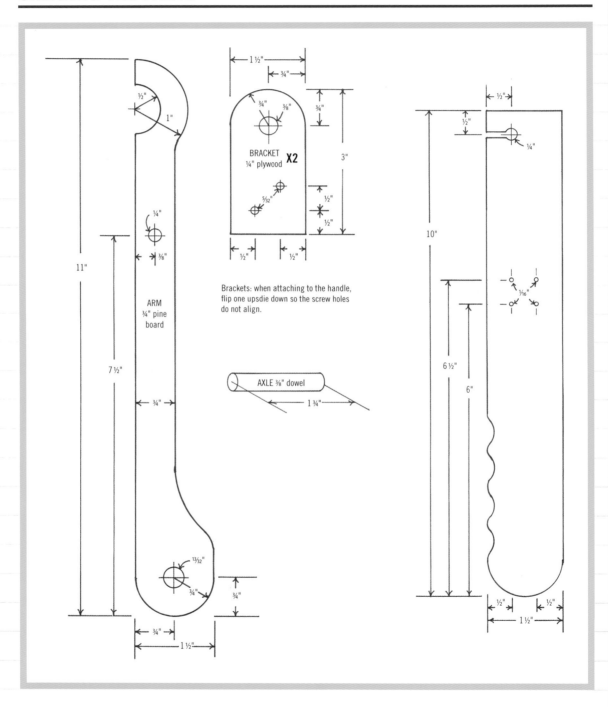

BRACKET
¼" plywood **X2**

ARM
¾" pine
board

Brackets: when attaching to the handle,
flip one upsdie down so the screw holes
do not align.

AXLE ⅜" dowel

# PUTTING IT ALL TOGETHER

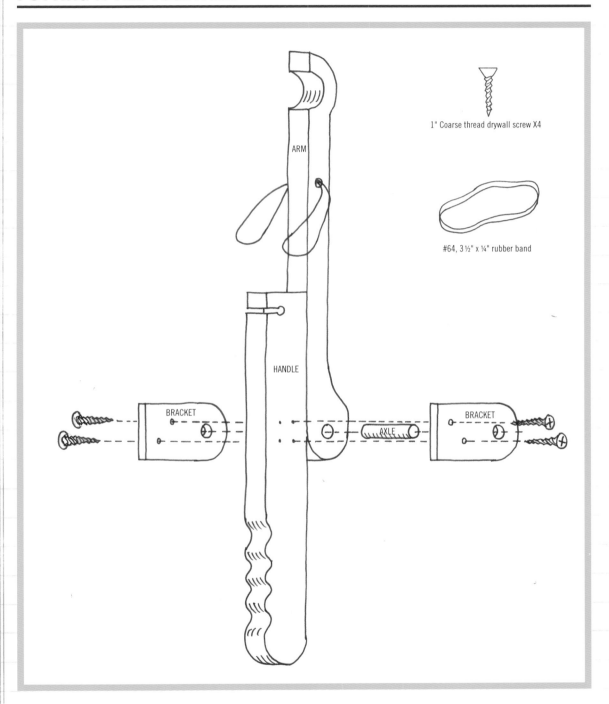

ARM

1" Coarse thread drywall screw X4

#64, 3 ½" x ¼" rubber band

HANDLE

BRACKET

BRACKET

AXLE

# HORIZONTAL WHEEL-TOP RACER

W e've all seen how fast a top can spin with the pull of a string. What will happen if we put the spinning top on its side? I imagine it would take off faster than sawdust up a vacuum—and that's mighty fast. Let's give it a try.

## MATERIALS

- ¾" x 1 ½" x 8"
  (2cm x 4cm x 20cm) pine board
- ¼" x 1 ½" x 4 ½"
  (6mm x 4cm x 11.5mm)
  pine board
- ¼" x 3" x 3"
  (6mm x 7.5cm x 7.5cm)
  plywood or pressed board
- ⅜" (1cm) dowel,
  2 ½" (6cm) long
- ¾" (2cm) dowel,
  2 ½" (6cm) long
- 2' (60cm) string
- 1 – #33, 3 ½ x ⅛" (9cm x 3mm)
  rubber band
- Glue (to keep the end of the string from fraying)

## TOOLS

- Drill with bits: ⅛" (3mm), ⅜" (1cm), ⁷⁄₁₆" (11mm)
- Scroll saw
- Tape measure
- Square
- Awl
- Pencil
- Scissors
- Compass
- Sandpaper

# PUTTING IT ALL TOGETHER

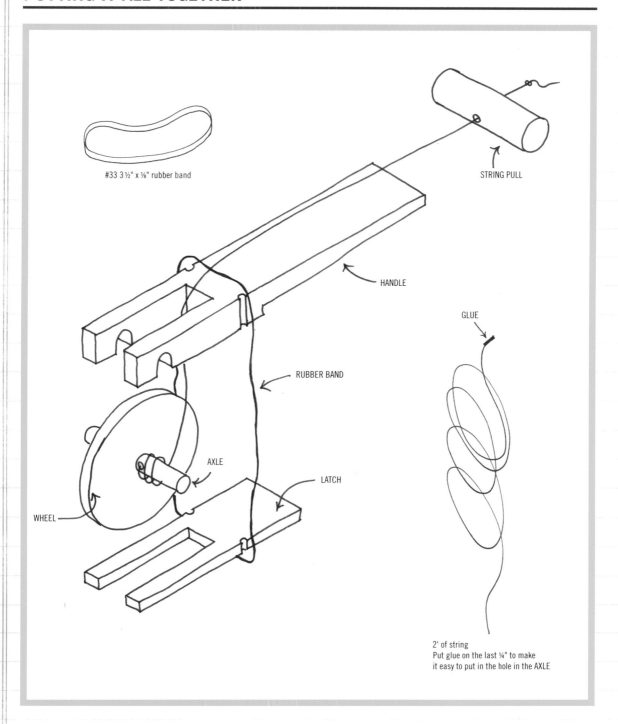

#33 3 ½" x ⅛" rubber band

STRING PULL

HANDLE

GLUE

RUBBER BAND

AXLE

LATCH

WHEEL

2' of string
Put glue on the last ¼" to make
it easy to put in the hole in the AXLE

# KNOCKER SHOOTER

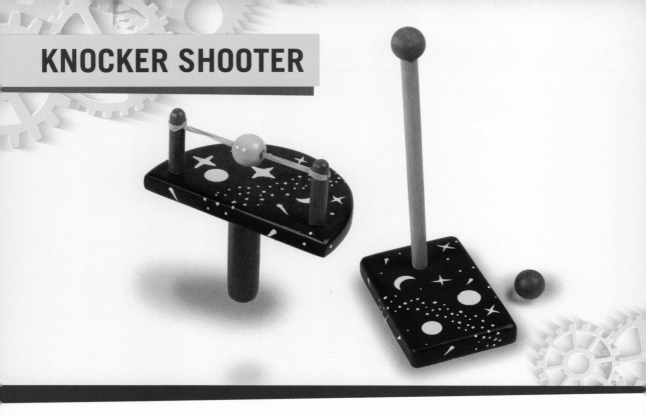

The game of billiards, or pool, has been around for hundreds of years and will likely be around for many more centuries. So what will this game look like on your trip to Mars with zero gravity? Imagine a billiards room with pockets in all 8 corners and in the center of all 6 walls. Balls will float around the room and the game will be played in three dimensions. We'd like to get a jump-start on becoming the first intergalactic pool champion, but nobody has invented an antigravity machine so we can practice. This simple toy, however, will add a third dimension to hitting balls around a room. Make "pockets" at different heights in boxes and create a 3D game of billiards.

## MATERIALS

- ¾" x 4" x 11 ½" (2cm x 10cm x 29cm) pine board
- ½" (13mm) dowel, 14" (36cm) long
- 1" (2.5cm) dowel, 4" (10cm) long
- 2 – 1" (2.5cm) wood balls
- 1 – #64, 3 ½" x ¼" (9cm x 6mm) rubber band
- Glue

## TOOLS

- Drill with bits: ¼" (6mm), ³⁄₁₆" (0.5cm), ⅜" (1cm), ½" (13mm), 1" (2.5cm)
- Scroll saw
- Tape measure
- Ruler
- Square
- Awl
- Pencil
- Scissors
- Compass
- Sandpaper
- Thin wire

# CUE BALL IN SPACE

The cue ball needs to move in a 3D space, but gravity wants to force it to the floor. We'll suspend our cue ball on a rubber band between two posts so it can move up, down, left, and right.

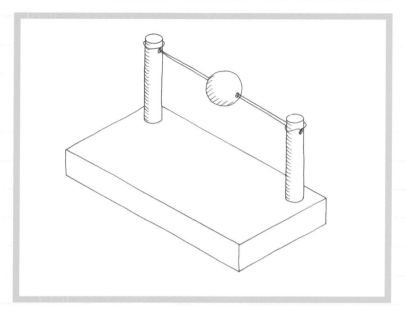

## PESKY GRAVITY

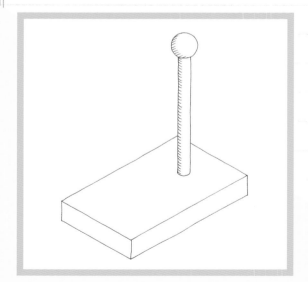

Our billiard balls should be floating but, once again, gravity keeps pulling them down. Our antigravity stick will hold them off the floor so we can hit them from below and knock them into the air.

## MAKESHIFT BILLIARD ROOM

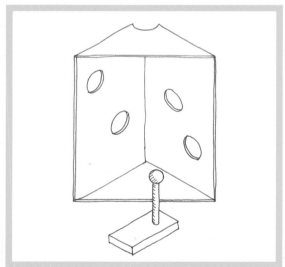

We're not floating around the billiard room so we'll make a quasi-3D billiards practice area. Cut a large box in half and make some holes in the top and sides for the pockets.

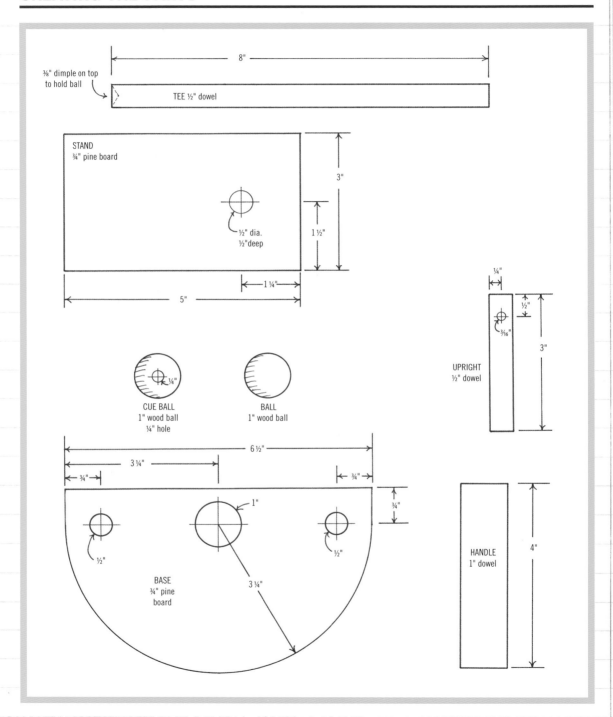

⅜" dimple on top to hold ball

TEE ½" dowel

8"

STAND
¾" pine board

3"

½" dia.
½" deep

1 ½"

1 ¼"

5"

CUE BALL
1" wood ball
¼" hole

BALL
1" wood ball

¼"

UPRIGHT
½" dowel

¼"

½"

3∕16"

3"

6 ½"

3 ¼"

¾"

¾"

1"

¾"

½"

½"

BASE
¾" pine
board

3 ¼"

HANDLE
1" dowel

4"

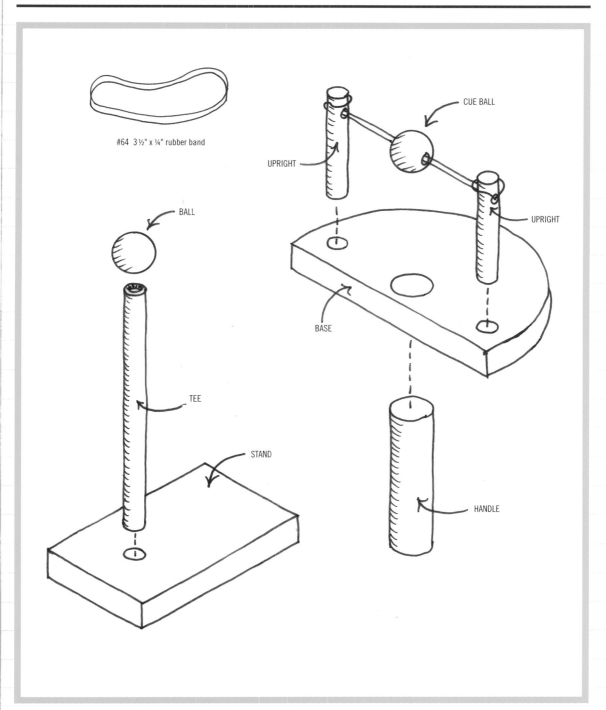

#64  3 ½" x ¼" rubber band

CUE BALL

UPRIGHT

UPRIGHT

BALL

BASE

TEE

STAND

HANDLE

# MOUSE ACROSS THE FLOOR

Even if you really like mice, snakes, and spiders, nothing triggers the "freak-out" zone of your brain like an unidentified, scurrying object running toward your feet. The purpose of this part of the brain is to make a person jump and squeal when they get surprised. To trigger that response, all we need to do is make something unexpectedly run at someone's feet. The scientific purpose of this project is to test family members' response time, jumping height, and squeal volume. But, of course, the real goal of this prank is to get a good chuckle.

## MATERIALS

- ¾" x 5 ½" x 20" (2cm x 14cm x 50mm) pine board
- ¼" x 3" x 6" (6mm x 7.5cm x 15cm) plywood board
- ¼" (6mm) dowel, 13 ½" (34cm) long
- 1 - 1" (2.5cm) wood sphere
- 8 – 1 ¼" (3cm) coarse-thread drywall screws
- 3 ½' (107cm) to 4' (122cm) string
- 2 – #33, 3 ½" x ⅛" (9cm x 3mm) rubber bands
- 1 – #4 x ⅜" (1cm) pan head Phillips screw (for attaching string to center)
- Glue
- Something that resembles a mouse, spider, snake, bug, or anything creepy

## TOOLS

- Drill with bits: ⁵⁄₃₂" (4mm), ¼" (6mm), ⁵⁄₁₆" (8mm), ⅜" (1cm)
- Phillips screwdriver
- Table saw or miter saw
- Scroll saw
- Tape measure
- Square
- Awl
- Pencil
- Scissors
- Compass

## THE MOUSE

Lucky for us, the "fight or flight" portion of our brain is much faster than the logic and thinking part. When suddenly startled, we will jump and scream long before the brain logically decides that there is nothing to fear. This means that our mouse can be made of anything and doesn't even have to look like a mouse.

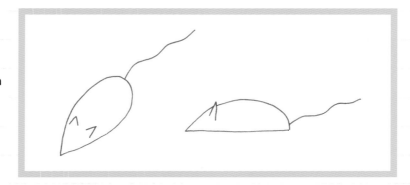

## RUNNING MOUSE

Just to keep it simple, a string will pull the mouse across the floor. A rubber band and spool will reel up the string.

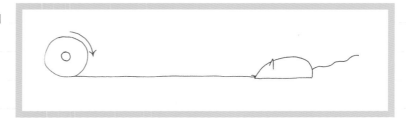

## TRIGGERING THE MOUSE

For this to be a total surprise, the mouse will run across the floor right after someone has opened a door. The victim's brain will think that the little critter was startled and may be trying to run up his pant leg. The door will unlatch the spool and send the mouse scurrying toward our unsuspecting victim's feet.

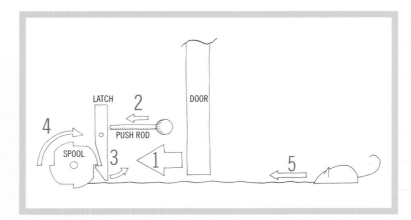

The rubber band can only stretch so far and then it breaks. The axle on the spool should be as thin as possible to get the most full-rotations of the spool. A ¼" (6mm) dowel is a good compromise between small diameter and strength.

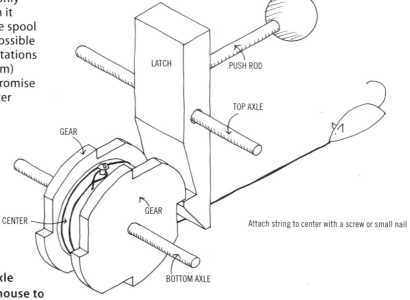

LATCH

PUSH ROD

TOP AXLE

GEAR

CENTER

GEAR

BOTTOM AXLE

Attach string to center with a screw or small nail

1. **Spin the bottom axle clockwise to pull mouse to the box.**

2. **Attach rubber band on the bottom axle as shown and tighten so it doesn't slip.**

3. **Loop rubber band over top axle.**

4. **Attach a second rubber band on the other side in the same way.**

¼" dia.

2 ¼" dia.

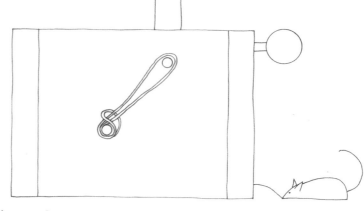

Circumference = π x D
Rubber band wraps around ¼" dowel = 5 x π x ¼" = 3.9"
String wraps around 2 ¼" spool = 5 x π x 2 ¼" = 35.3"

# CREATING THE PARTS

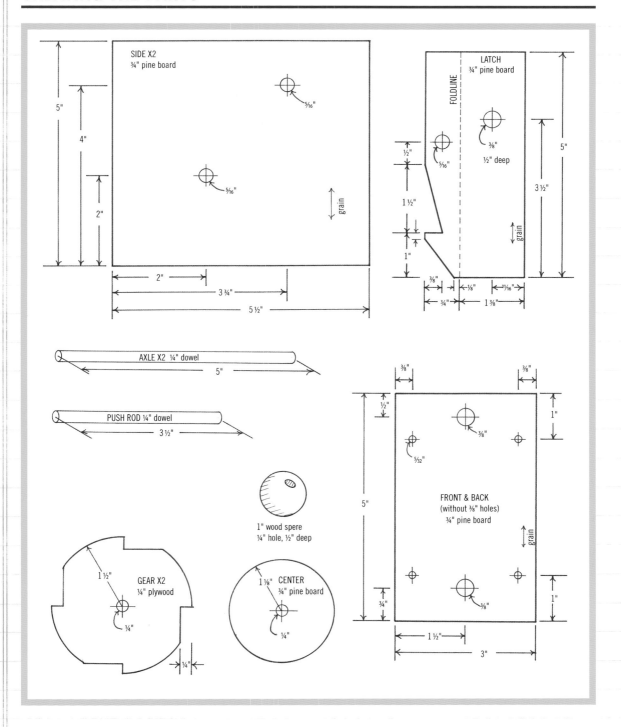

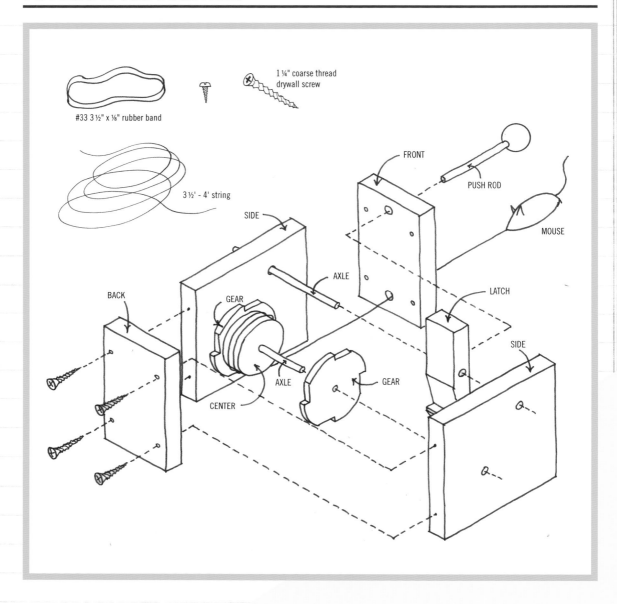

#33 3 ½" x ⅛" rubber band

1 ¼" coarse thread drywall screw

3 ½' - 4' string

FRONT

PUSH ROD

MOUSE

SIDE

AXLE

LATCH

BACK

GEAR

SIDE

AXLE

GEAR

CENTER

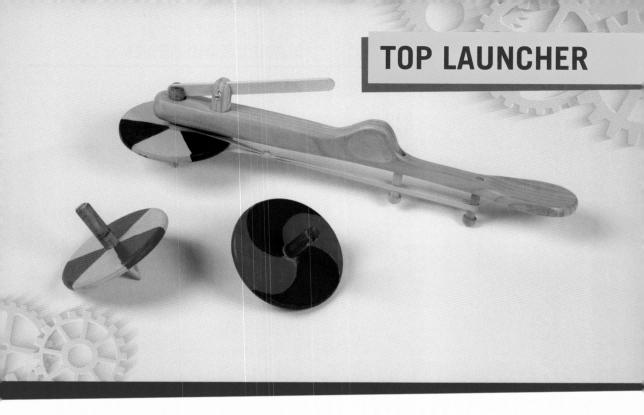

# TOP LAUNCHER

**T**ops are fascinating for their crazy ability to balance on one tiny point seeming to defy gravity. They can spin across a flat surface for such a lengthy time. Most astounding, they don't get dizzy. One top whirling across the floor mesmerizes us. Wouldn't a swarm of tops all dancing together be totally amazing? Only one way to find out: we need to invent a top launcher and then connect a whole bunch of them together.

## MATERIALS
- ¾" x ¾" x 10" (2cm x 2cm x 25cm) pine board
- ½" (13mm) dowel, 1 ½" (4cm) long
- ⅜" (1cm) dowel, 2 ½" (6cm) long
- ¼" x 3" x 3" (6mm x 7.5cm x 7.5cm) pine or plywood board
- 1 craft stick
- 2 – ¼" (6mm) pegs, 1" (2.5cm) long
- #20 x ¾" (2cm) wire nail
- 1 – #64, 3" x ¼" (7.5cm x 6mm) rubber band

## TOOLS
- Drill with bits: ¹⁄₁₆" (1.5mm), ⁷⁄₃₂" (0.5cm), ⅜" (1cm), ⁷⁄₁₆" (11mm), ½" (13mm)
- Scroll saw
- Hammer
- Tape measure
- Square
- Awl
- Pencil
- Scissors
- Compass
- Sandpaper

## TRADITIONAL TOP LAUNCHER

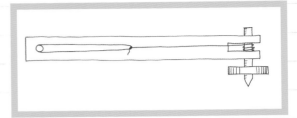

The most familiar way to launch a top is with a string wound around the shaft. A quick pull sends the top spinning.

## RUBBER BAND POWER

We can't pull lots of strings at the same time, so let's try using a rubber band to pull the string.

## RUBBER BAND—ROUND 2

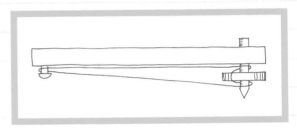

The rubber band can't stretch far enough to pull the string, so the first attempt didn't work. How about just winding the rubber band around the shaft— forget the string. Wow! This works amazingly well. One loop of the rubber band really sends the top spinning.

## THE LATCH

Now we need a way to prevent the top from spinning while we get the other tops ready for launch. A thin slot in the top of shaft will act as a latch.

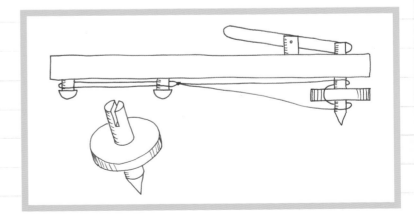

# IMPROVEMENT

The rubber band snaps your fingers (Ouch!) and falls off the peg (frustrating) on every launch. You can fix this painful and annoying problem by tying a knot in the middle of the rubber band and adding a second peg.

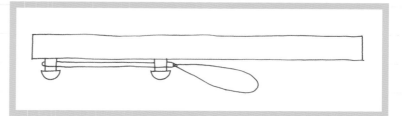

Pull rubber band far past the top with the top in the loop.

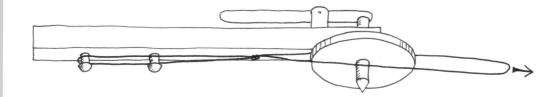

Wrap the rubber band on the shaft and release. This is the launch position.

## TOPS, TOPS, EVERYWHERE!

This single top launcher is now left in your capable hands. Go invent a way to put 10 of these together to release a swarm of tops.

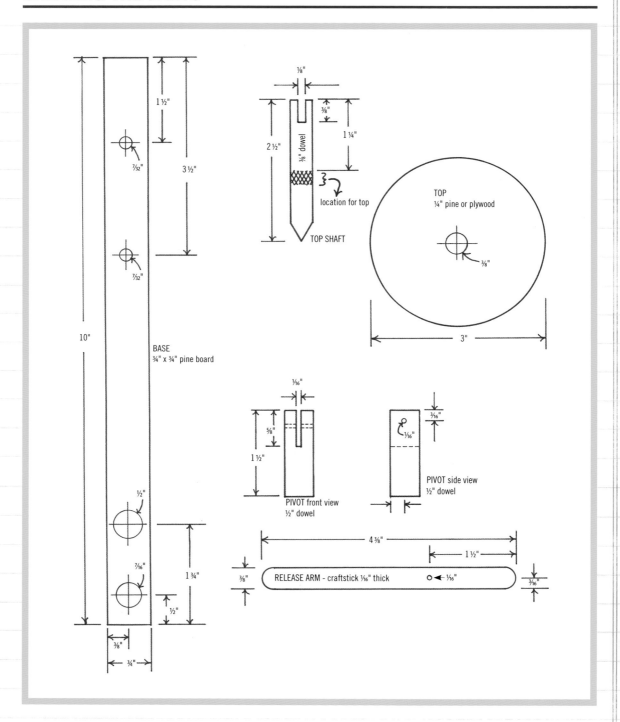

1 ½"

3 ½"

10"

⁷/₃₂"

⁷/₃₂"

½"

⁷/₁₆"

BASE
¾" x ¾" pine board

1 ¾"

½"

³/₈"

¾"

⅛"

2 ½"

³/₈"

1 ¼"

³/₈" dowel

location for top

TOP SHAFT

TOP
¼" pine or plywood

³/₈"

3"

¹/₁₆"

⅝"

1 ½"

PIVOT front view
½" dowel

³/₁₆"

¹/₁₆"

PIVOT side view
½" dowel

4 ³/₈"

1 ½"

³/₈"

RELEASE ARM - craftstick ¹/₁₆" thick

¹/₁₆"

³/₁₆"

# PUTTING IT ALL TOGETHER

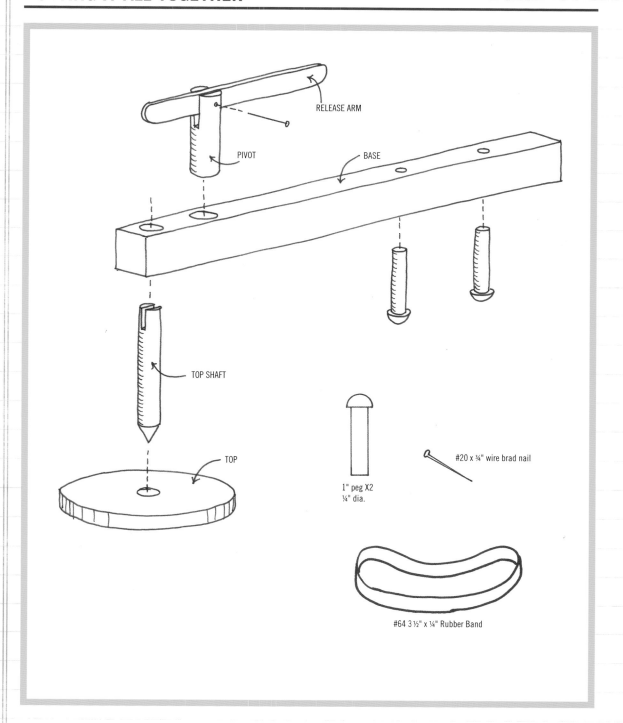

RELEASE ARM

PIVOT

BASE

TOP SHAFT

TOP

1" peg X2
¼" dia.

#20 x ¾" wire brad nail

#64 3 ½" x ¼" Rubber Band

# CATAPULT CASTLE

## MATERIALS

- Pine, ¾" (2cm) thick:
  - 2 – 3 ½" x 11 ½" (9cm x 29cm) sides
  - 3 ½" x 6" (9cm x 15cm) trigger
  - 1 ½" x 5" (4cm x 13cm) striker
  - ¾" x 11 ¼" (2cm x 29cm) spacers and battlements
- Plywood, ¼" (6mm) thick:
  - 4" x 5" (10cm x 13cm) top
  - 4" x 2" (10cm x 5cm) front
- Dowels:
  - ⅜" (1cm) diameter x 9" (23cm)
  - ½" (13mm) diameter x 1" (2.5cm)
- 1 ½" (4cm) wooden ball
- 6 – 1" coarse-thread drywall screws
- 1 – #64, 3 ½" x ¼" (9cm x 6mm) rubber band
- 1 – Ping-Pong® ball
- Glue: wood glue, hot glue, and spray adhesive or glue stick for patterns
- Paint: brown stain, neutral gray, white, black

## TOOLS

- Drill with bits 5⁄32" (4mm), ⅜" (1cm), 7⁄16" (11mm), ½" (13mm), 1 ½" (4cm), and countersink
- Phillips screwdriver
- Table or miter saw
- Scroll saw
- Coping saw
- Tape measure
- 45º Triangle, square
- Compass
- Awl
- Pencil
- Scissors
- Broad and fine-tip paintbrushes
- Toothbrush
- Sandpaper

L ay siege to the castle by breaking down the portcullis with a battering ram but keep a wary eye, for the king and his men have a mighty catapult that can hurl gigantic boulders at you and your knights. Translation: roll a ball into the castle's portcullis and the king retaliates by launching a Ping-Pong® ball back at you. Defend yourself with a homemade shield and sword or try to catch the massive stone to show the king just how fast and strong you really are.

*In days of old,*
*when woodworkers were bold,*

*no electricity in their castle,*
*hand-powered tools were all they had,*
*it really was a hassle.*

*They cut and drilled with their*
*own strength,*

*and built with hands so callous.*

*Oh, it was a stirring sight,*
*these craftsmen in the palace.*

(Inspired by Jimmy Buffett's song "Gypsies in the Palace")

## RETHINK THE CATAPULT

Catapults use a long arm to hurl heavy boulders. A long arm will make our castle a little too big. However, since we are just using lightweight Ping-Pong balls, we can shorten the arm and make it smack the ball rather than throw it.

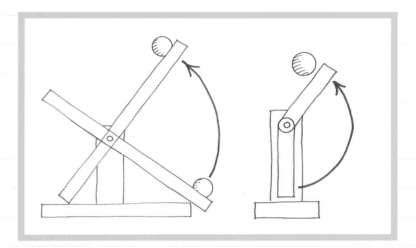

## HOLDING THE BALL

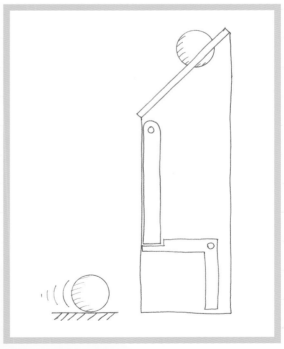

We will hold the ball at an angle of 45° for maximum distance.

## A LATCH

A simple latch will hold the striker ready until our attack ball releases it.

# A BETTER LATCH

After launching, the latch falls down and makes reloading difficult because it takes two hands to reset. If we add a weight to the back of the latch, it will be in the right position for reloading and will automatically engage the striker.

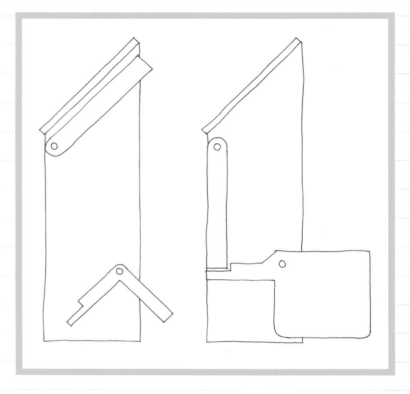

# CREATING THE PARTS

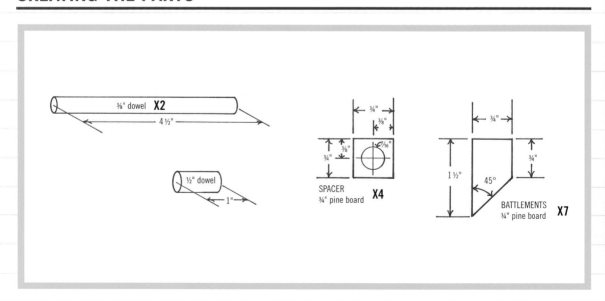

⅜" dowel **X2**

4 ½"

½" dowel

1"

¾"
⅜"
⁷⁄₁₆"
⅜"
¾"
SPACER
¾" pine board **X4**

¾"
1 ½"
45°
¾"
BATTLEMENTS
¾" pine board **X7**

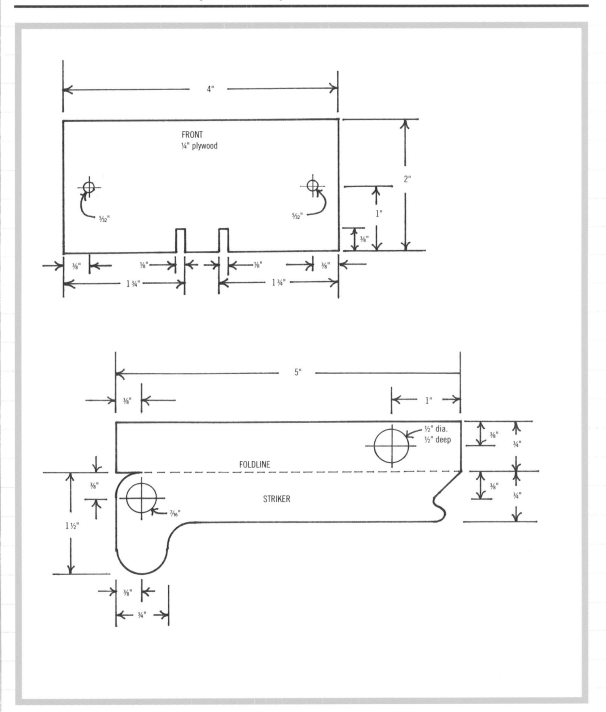

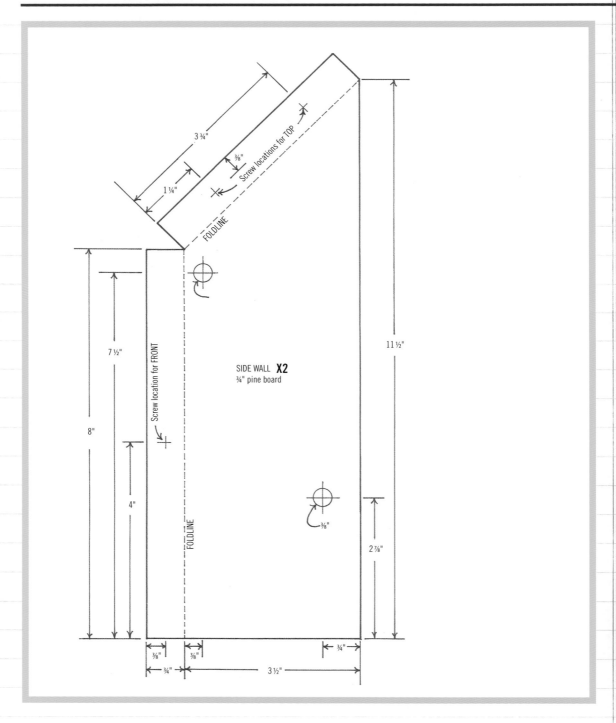

SIDE WALL **X2**
¾" pine board

Screw locations for TOP

Screw location for FRONT

FOLDLINE

FOLDLINE

3 ¾"

1 ¼"

⅜"

11 ½"

7 ½"

8"

4"

2 ⅞"

⅜"

⅜"

⅜"

¾"

¾"

¾"

3 ½"

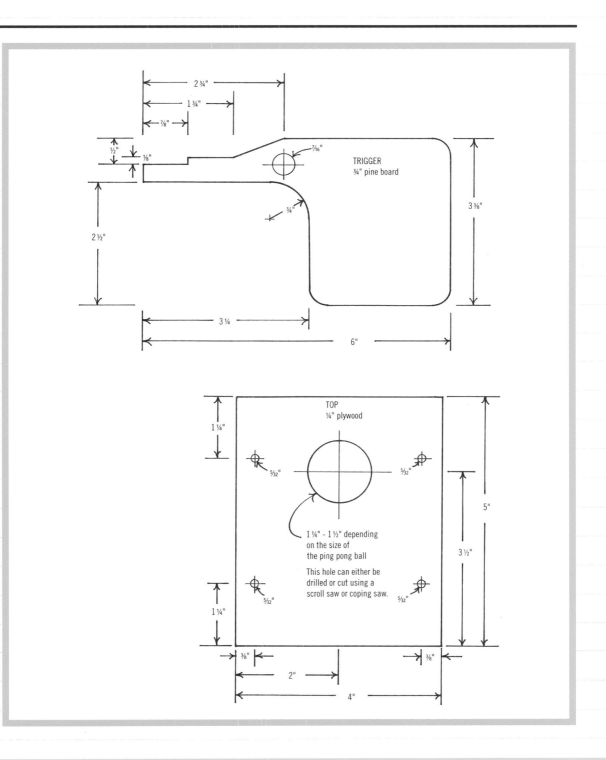

2 ¾"

1 ¾"

⅞"

½"

⅛"

⁷⁄₁₆"

TRIGGER
¾" pine board

3 ⅜"

¾"

2 ½"

3 ¼

6"

TOP
¼" plywood

1 ¼"

⁵⁄₃₂"

⁵⁄₃₂"

1 ¼" - 1 ½" depending
on the size of
the ping pong ball

This hole can either be
drilled or cut using a
scroll saw or coping saw.

⁵⁄₃₂"

⁵⁄₃₂"

1 ¼"

5"

3 ½"

⅜"

⅜"

2"

4"

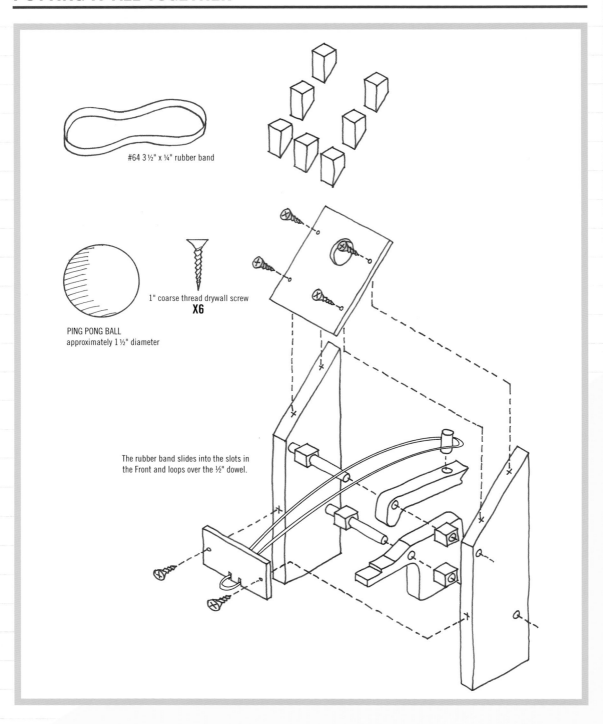

#64 3 ½" x ¼" rubber band

1" coarse thread drywall screw
**X6**

PING PONG BALL
approximately 1 ½" diameter

The rubber band slides into the slots in
the Front and loops over the ½" dowel.

# RIGHT BACK ATCHA

## MATERIALS

- ¾" x 5 ½" x 24"
  (2cm x 14cm x 61cm) pine board
- ¾" x 3 ⅜" x 15"
  (2cm x 8.5cm x 38cm) pine board
- ¾" x 2" x 34"
  (2cm x 5cm x 86cm) pine board
- ¾" x 1" x 5"
  (2cm x 2.5cm x 13m) pine board
- ¼" x 5 ¼" x 9"
  (6mm x 13cm x 23cm) plywood
- ⅜" (1cm) dowel, 30" (76cm) long
- ½" (13mm) dowel,
  4" (10cm) long
- 4 – 1" (2.5cm) pegs
- 4 – 1" (2.5cm) coarse-thread
  drywall screws
- 4 – 1 ¼" (3cm) coarse-thread
  drywall screws
- 5 - #32 3" x ⅛" (7.5cm x 3mm)
  rubber bands

## TOOLS

- Drill with bits: ⁵⁄₃₂" (4mm),
  ⁷⁄₃₂" (5mm), ⅜" (1cm),
  ⁷⁄₁₆" (11mm), ½" (13mm),
  counter sink
- Phillips screwdriver
- Table saw
- Scroll saw
- Miter saw
- Hammer
- Tape measure
- Square
- Awl
- Pencil
- Scissors
- 45° triangle
- Compass
- Sandpaper

**T**he Catapult Castle project (see page 80) was loads of fun and inspired several new games with points for launching and more points for catching. We wanted to ramp up the fun by adding more castles. That's where this project began, by heading into the shop to build 4 more castles.

## WOOD SUPPLIES

The first idea was to just make 4 more castles. However, we quickly realized that there was not enough wood in the shop. Not wanting to delay the project with a run to the lumberyard, we redefined the project. The idea of 4 separate castles was replaced with a wider castle with more catapults. Now only 2 sides were needed.

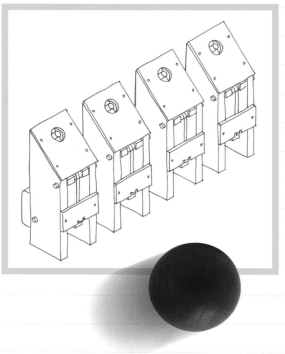

## MORE CATAPULTS

Adding more catapults required doing a little math to figure out the spacing between them. The Ping-Pong® balls are roughly 1 ½" (13mm) diameter, and there needed to be about ¼" (6mm) between the balls. Here's the math: 1 ⅞" + 1 ¾" + 1 ¾" + 1 ¾" + 1 ⅞" = 9" (4.75cm + 4.5cm + 4.5cm + 4.5cm + 4.75cm = 23cm).

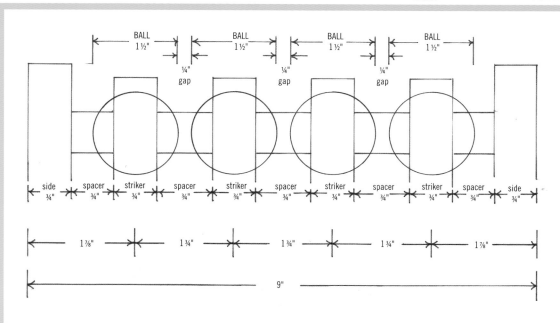

## THE BIG DISAPPOINTMENT

The project was completed, rubber bands installed, and 4 Ping-Pong® balls were loaded. The excitement was high anticipating hours of fun with the new toy. However, the invention process often reveals things that were not taken into consideration. In this case it was the jarring action from the first Ping-Pong® ball launched. The shock dislodged all the other Ping-Pong® balls, and they'd just dribble to the floor.

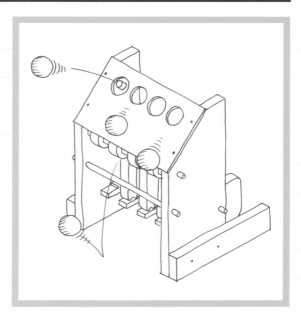

## THE FINAL FIX

The project went on hold for several months until the idea to use rubber bands popped up. By just adding a few pegs and another rubber band, the project came back to life and worked better than ever.

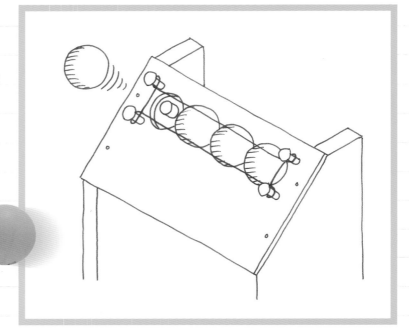

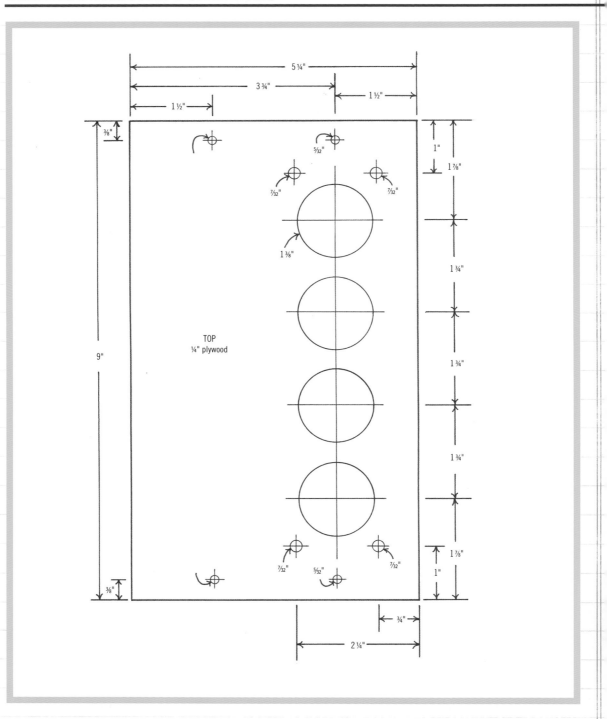

TOP
¼" plywood

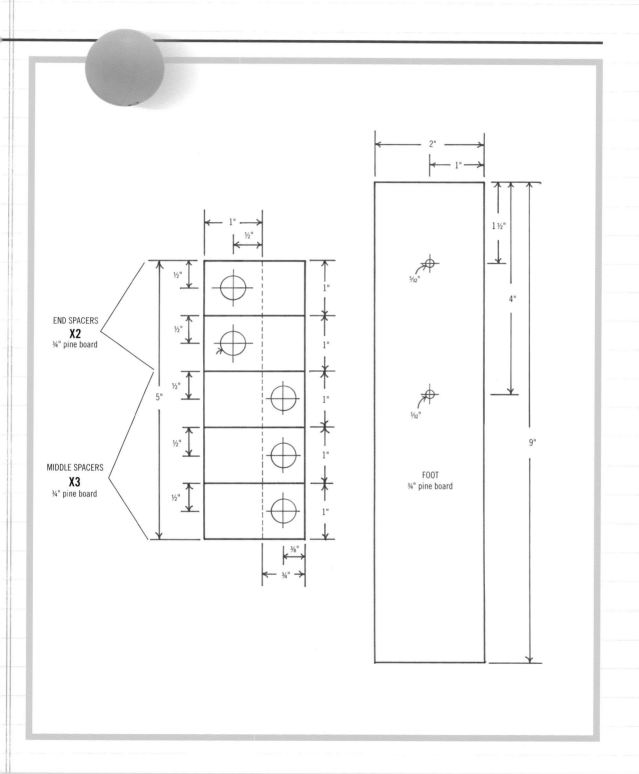

END SPACERS
**X2**
¾" pine board

MIDDLE SPACERS
**X3**
¾" pine board

FOOT
¾" pine board

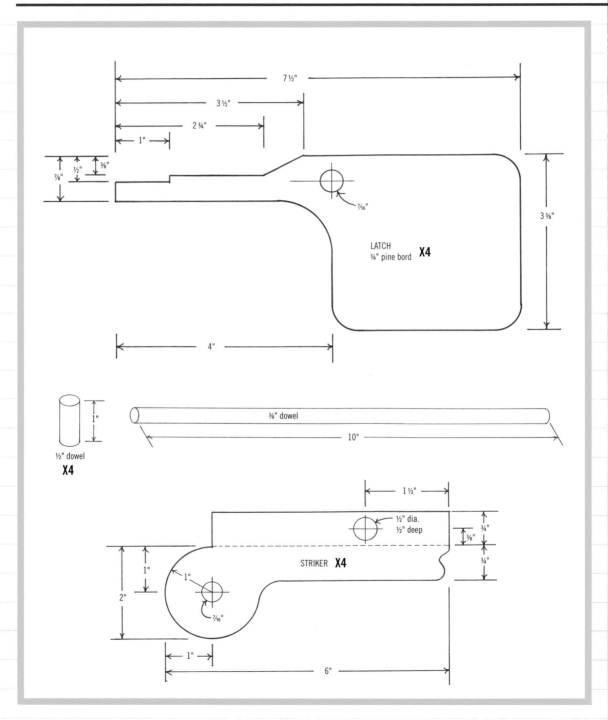

7 ½"

3 ½"

2 ¾"

1"

⅜"

½"

⅞"

3 ⅜"

7/16"

LATCH
¾" pine bord **X4**

4"

1"

½" dowel
**X4**

⅜" dowel

10"

1 ½"

½" dia.
½" deep

¾"

⅜"

¾"

STRIKER **X4**

1"

1"

2"

7/16"

1"

6"

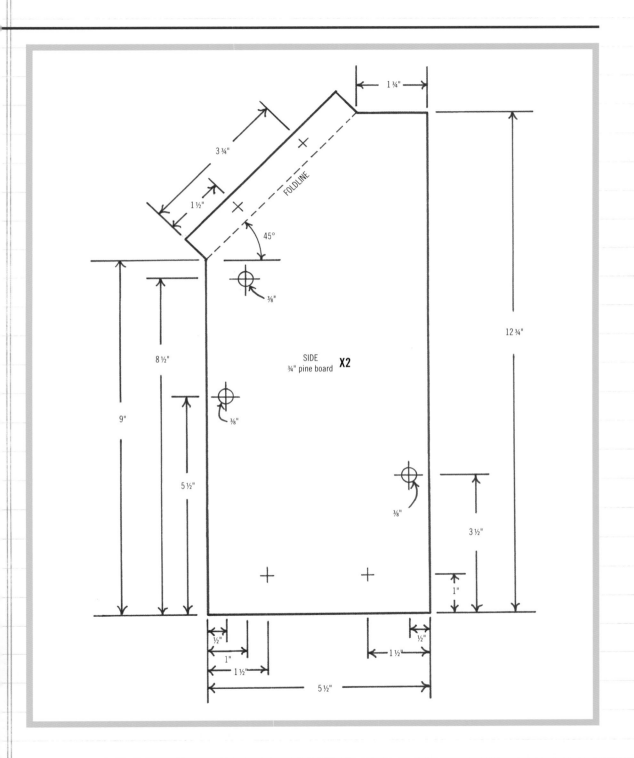

SIDE
¾" pine board **X2**

FOLDLINE

45°

1 ¾"
3 ¾"
1 ½"
⅜"
⅜"
12 ¾"
8 ½"
9"
5 ½"
3 ½"
⅜"
1"
½"
1"
1 ½"
1 ½"
½"
5 ½"

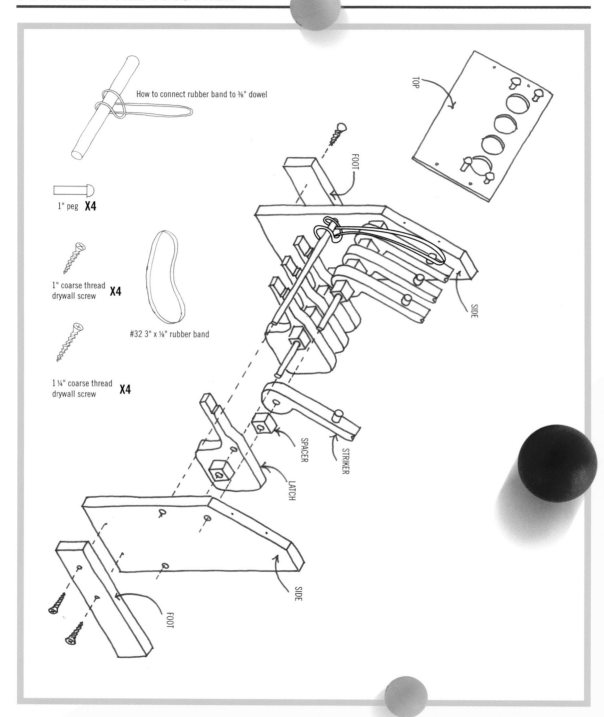

How to connect rubber band to ⅜" dowel

1" peg **X4**

1" coarse thread drywall screw **X4**

#32 3" x ⅛" rubber band

1 ¼" coarse thread drywall screw **X4**

TOP

FOOT

SIDE

SPACER

STRIKER

LATCH

SIDE

FOOT

# CUP & BALL (WITHOUT THE STRING)

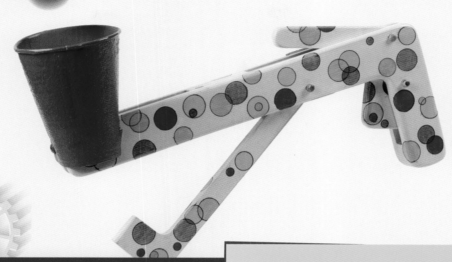

The cup and ball is a classic toy that kids played with while they waited for electricity and videos games to be invented. You've probably seen one before: it's simply a ball on a string connected to a cup. The challenge comes from trying to flip the ball into the air and catch it in the cup. Not nearly as easy as you'd think. The only drawback is that this toy is just so old-fashioned. It's time to add a modern twist and a lot more excitement to this classic.

## REQUIREMENTS FOR 21ST-CENTURY CUP & BALL

**1.** Keep the basics: A cup and a ball

**2.** No strings attached: Bounce the ball off the wall if you want to.

**3.** A launcher: Launch a ball as high as you want.

**4.** The first two are easy, but the third will take some serious thinking!

## WHAT IT SHOULD LOOK LIKE

The first plan is to have just a cup on top of a handle with a trigger.

## TRIGGER

The first version looks like this. If you're thinking there's no way you can pull the trigger fast enough to launch a ball, then you are correct. I should have asked you before building one.

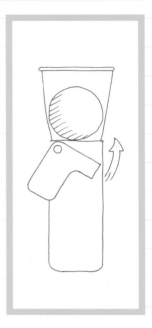

## THE NEED FOR SPEED

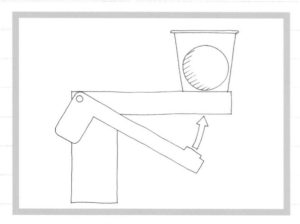

The easiest way to get more speed from the hammer is to just extend the arm. This becomes a very awkward toy because the trigger is in the wrong direction.

## TURN IT AROUND

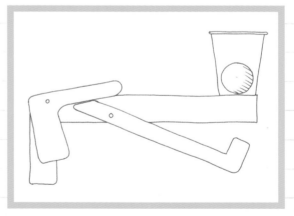

To get the hammer facing forward, it needs to be disconnected from the trigger. Now when we pull the trigger a short distance, the hammer will move a long distance in the same amount of time—that is, it moves much faster. Now we can pop a ball high into the sky, and with a little practice, scoop it out of the air with the cup.

## ATTACHING THE CUP

Cut out a rectangle from the side of the cup and remove the bottom.

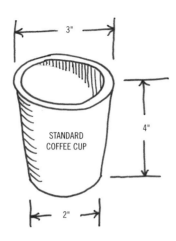

STANDARD
COFFEE CUP

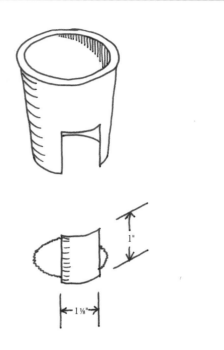

Fit the cup over the end of the handles. Use an awl to mark a starter hole in the cup and one handle.

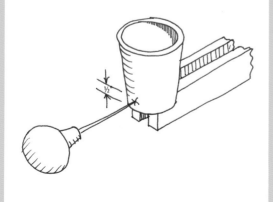

Attach the cup to the handle with the screw.

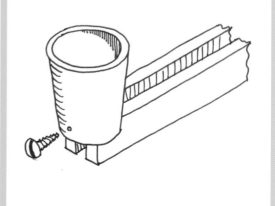

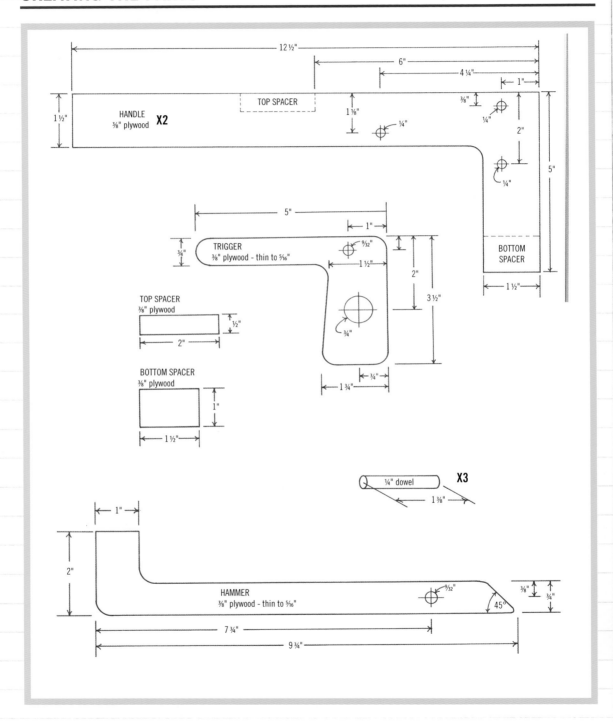

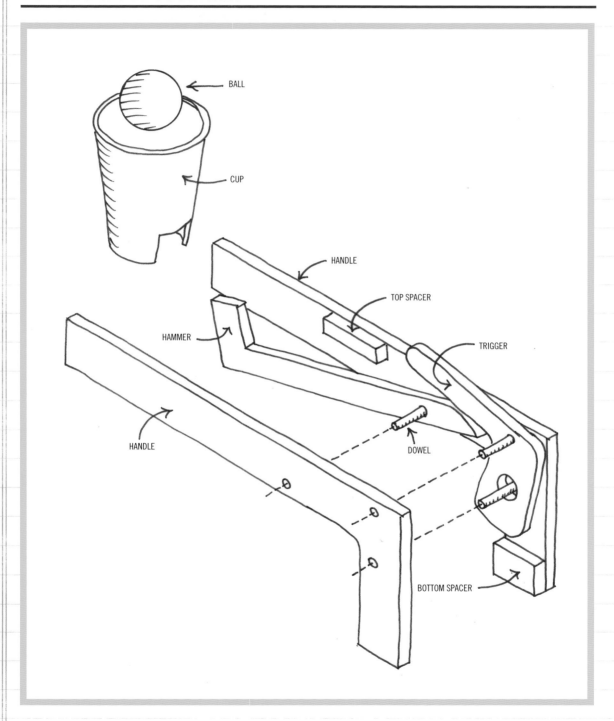

BALL

CUP

HANDLE

TOP SPACER

HAMMER

TRIGGER

HANDLE

DOWEL

BOTTOM SPACER

# TREASURE-HUNT BOX

**Y**ou never know what you'll unearth when you dig for treasure. Most times you will find an empty hole, but once in a while your shovel will hit metal—"clink!"—and soon fascinating treasures and ancient artifacts will be uncovered. This toy captures that exciting moment of discovering something unexpected. Let loose your inner treasure hunter and dig around for a while. There won't be a mess, and there won't be any holes to fill.

## MATERIALS
- 1 ½" x 4" x 41"
  (4cm x 10cm x 104cm) pine board
- 8 ¾" x 8 ¾" x ¼"
  (22cm x 22cm x 6mm) plywood
- 8 ¾" x 8 ¾" x ⅛"
  (22cm x 22cm x 3mm) acrylic
- 2 – 1 ½" (4cm) diameter wooden balls
- ⅜" (1cm) dowel, 24" (61cm) long
- ¼" (6mm) dowel, 18" (46cm) long
- ⅛" (3mm) dowel, 3 ¼" (8cm) long
- ¾" x 1 ½" x 2 ¾"
  (2cm x 4cm x 7cm) pine board for shovel and rake
- 8 – 2" coarse-thread drywall screws
- 11,000 fuse beads or any craft bead larger than ⅜" (1cm) diameter to fill the box 1 ¼" (3cm) deep *(Did I count these? No, that's what the box said.)*
- Glue
- Treasures, trinkets, knick-knacks, flotsam, and jetsam

## TOOLS
- Drill with bits: ⅛" (3mm), ⁵⁄₃₂" (4mm), ¼" (6mm), ⅜" (1cm), ⁷⁄₁₆" (11mm), 1 ½" (4cm), counter sink
- Phillips screwdriver
- Table saw
- Scroll saw
- Hammer
- Tape measure
- Square
- Awl
- Pencil
- Scissors
- Sandpaper
- Rotary tools with barrel sander

## SEALED BOX

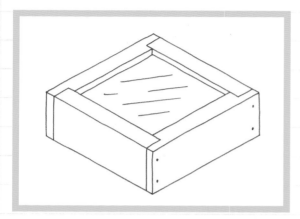

We don't want to make a mess, so we will design a box with a clear lid to hold our "dirt."

## TREASURE-HUNTING TOOLS

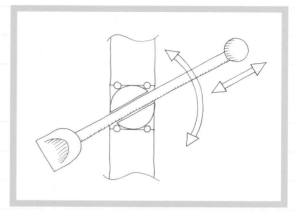

A shovel is absolutely necessary, and a rake would also be very useful. The tools need to move in three dimensions to reach anywhere in our box. This will be accomplished with a ball joint so the dirt doesn't spill out.

## THE "DIRT"

Choosing the best "dirt" is done by trial and error:

- **Backyard dirt:** No good. Small rocks jammed the ball joint.

- **Colored sand:** Colorful but it made the ball joint hard to move, and it seeped out of box.

- **Pinto beans:** A little bulky, but no jamming. Bland looking.

- **Plastic beads:** Works great! No jamming and very colorful.

Fill the box with interesting little knick-knacks and trinkets. Perhaps write a story around the items or create a treasure-hunting game.

## HELPFUL HINTS

- Taper the eight ¼" (6mm) dowels so they can be easily inserted and removed from the holes during construction.
- If the wooden ball does not rotate smoothly in the 1 ½" (4cm) hole, use a rotary tool with a barrel sander to slightly enlarge the hole. The balls are likely not perfectly round.
- Make the ⅛" (3mm) and ¼" (6mm) grooves for the top and bottom slightly wider so there's no binding. This will allow a small amount of misalignment during assembly.
- If you paint the box, be careful not to get any paint on the ball or it may get stuck.

# CREATING THE PARTS

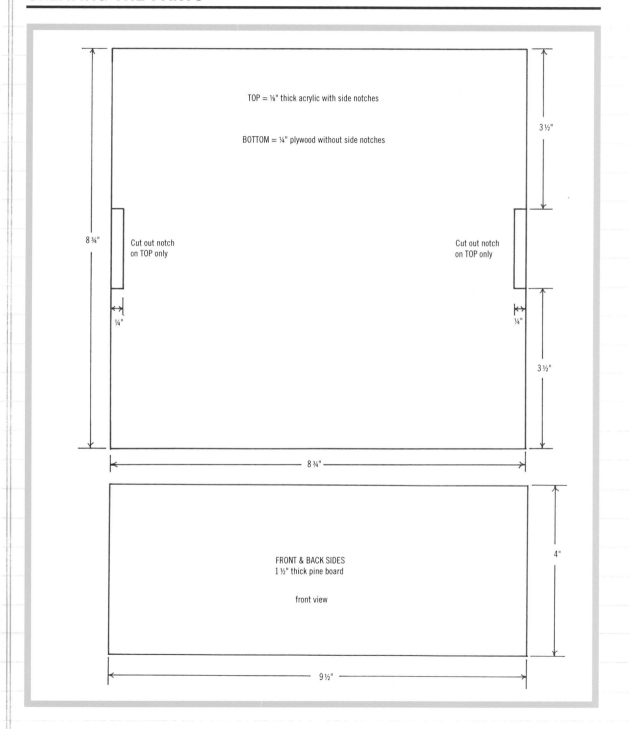

TOP = ⅛" thick acrylic with side notches

BOTTOM = ¼" plywood without side notches

8 ¾"

Cut out notch
on TOP only

Cut out notch
on TOP only

3 ½"

3 ½"

¼"

¼"

8 ¾"

FRONT & BACK SIDES
1 ½" thick pine board

front view

4"

9 ½"

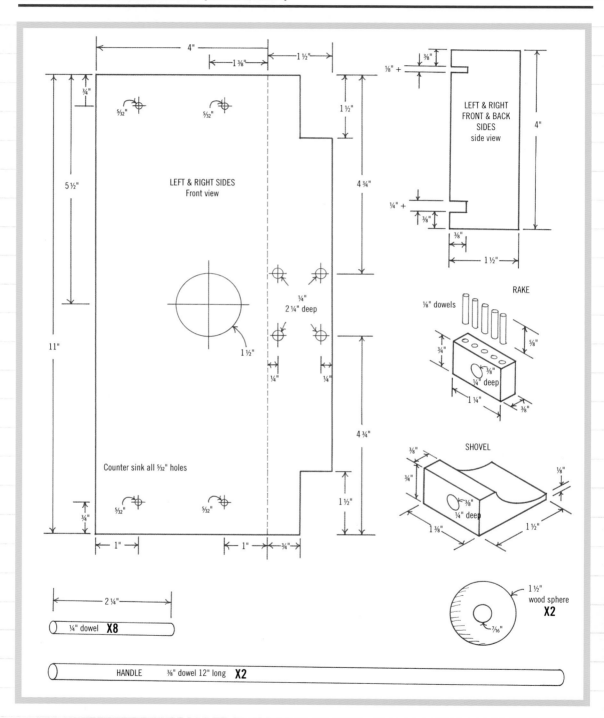

LEFT & RIGHT SIDES
Front view

Counter sink all 5/32" holes

LEFT & RIGHT
FRONT & BACK
SIDES
side view

RAKE

1/8" dowels

SHOVEL

1/4" dowel **X8**

HANDLE     3/8" dowel 12" long **X2**

1 1/2"
wood sphere
**X2**

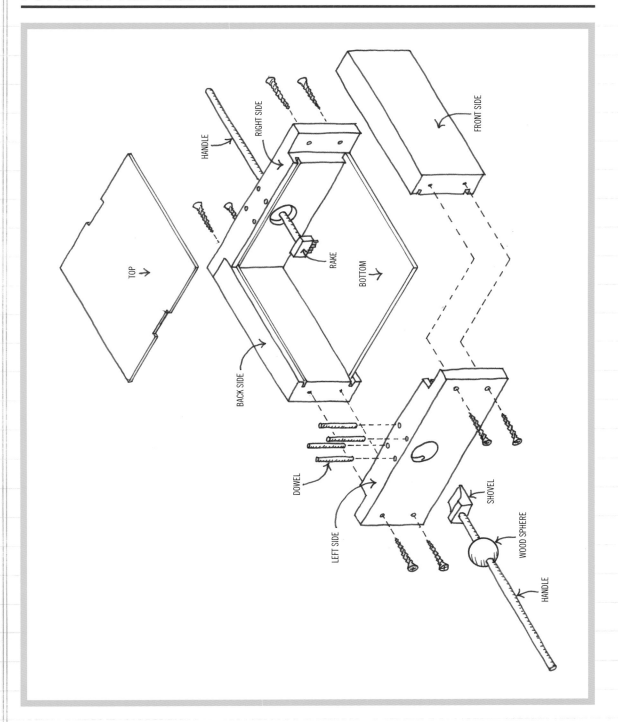

HANDLE

RIGHT SIDE

FRONT SIDE

TOP →

RAKE

BOTTOM →

BACK SIDE

DOWEL

LEFT SIDE

SHOVEL

WOOD SPHERE

HANDLE

# "IS IT WORTH IT?" GIFT BOX

**G**ive the gift that begs the question, "Is it worth it?" Just a simple box, but getting it open is going to require most of the tools on the workbench. Is there a final reward inside for rising to the challenge or just a note wondering why it took so long? So decide how devious you want to be and have fun.

## MATERIALS
- ¾" x 4 ½" x 30" (2cm x 11.5cm x 76cm) pine board
- Screws, bolts, nuts, nails, duct tape, wire, tie wraps, staples, string, rope, etc.

## TOOLS
- Scroll saw
- Tape measure
- Square
- Pencil
- Others tools as needed: drill, bits, screwdrivers, wrench, pliers, wire cutter, hammer

## SIMPLE BOX

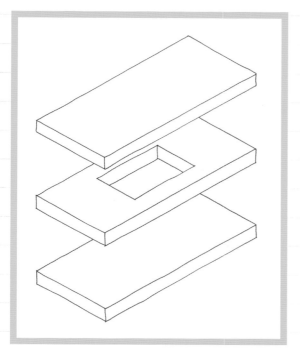

Only the simplest box is needed and it doesn't have to hold more than a gift card. That will leave lots of room to add torment.

## CLOSING THE BOX

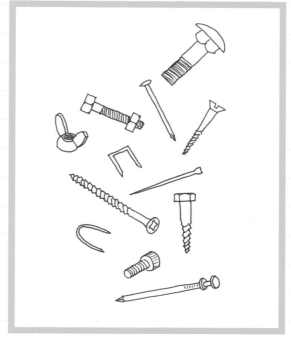

This is a great time to survey the shop and find all the leftover fasteners from various projects: nails, nuts and bolts, screws, wires, tie wraps, duct tape, etc. Glue? Naw, that's too mean. Make sure multiple tools are needed and then go to town putting the box together. Don't forget to put in the gift, or you'll be deciding if it's worth it.

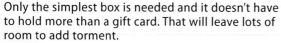

## A LEARNING EXPERIENCE

Remember, you will likely be helping with the disassembly, but what a great opportunity to teach about different tools.

# CREATING THE PARTS

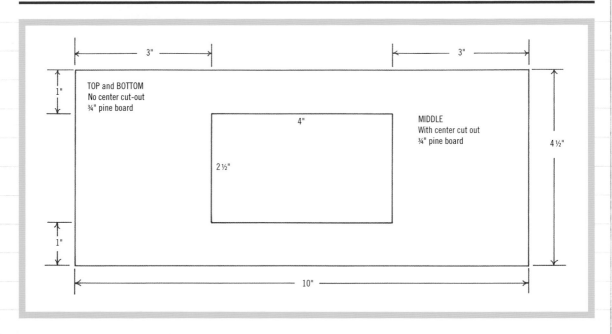

3"                                    3"

1"

TOP and BOTTOM
No center cut-out
¾" pine board

4"

MIDDLE
With center cut out
¾" pine board

4 ½"

2 ½"

1"

10"

# PUTTING IT ALL TOGETHER

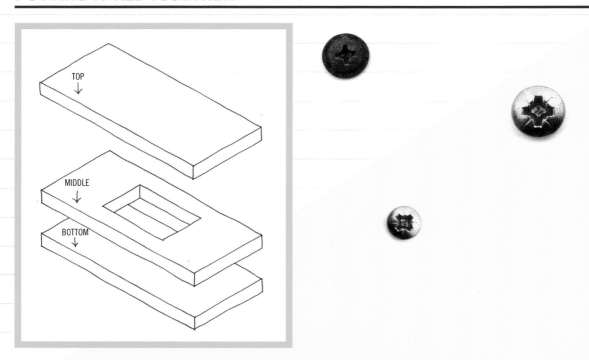

TOP
↓

MIDDLE
↓

BOTTOM
↓

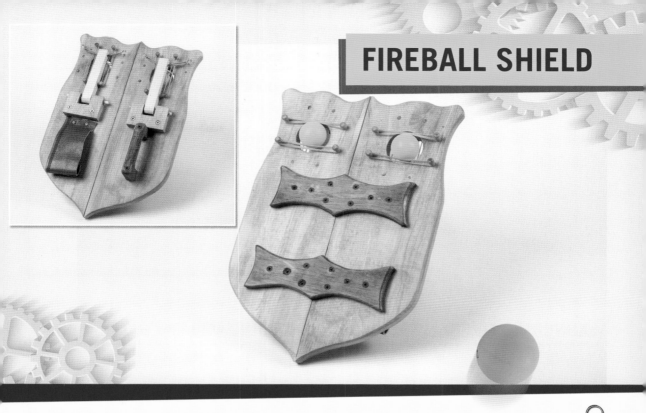

# FIREBALL SHIELD

A shield, a sword, and a courageous heart are the only weapons a knight uses to slay dragons. If my knightly duty is to protect villagers by seeking out ferocious, fire-breathing, flying lizards, then I'd definitely spend lots of time inventing contraptions that put more distance between me and the beast's fiery breath and huge claws. Swords are great, but to be effective you have to get much closer to a dragon than I like. How about creating a shield that not only defends but also launches an attack?

## MATERIALS

- ¾" x 5 ½" x 43" (2cm x 14cm x 109cm) pine board
- ½" x 5" x 8" (13mm x 13mm x 20cm) plywood
- ¼" (6mm) dowel, 7" (18cm) long
- 2 ½" x 8" (6cm x 20cm) canvas or leather
- 2 – 2 ½" (6cm) coarse-thread drywall screws
- 4 – 1 ¼" (3cm) coarse-thread drywall screws
- 16 – ¾" (2cm) coarse-thread drywall screws
- 4 – 1" (2.5cm) hook screws
- 4 – #10 - ½" (13mm) pan head screw
- 16 – 1" (2.5cm) pegs
- 10 – #33 3 ½" x ⅛" (9cm x 3mm) rubber bands
- 2 – Ping-Pong® balls

## TOOLS

- Drill with bits: 5⁄32" (4mm), 3⁄16" (4.5mm), 7⁄32" (5mm), ¼" (6mm), 9⁄32" (7mm), counter sink, 2" (5cm) hole cutter (or use scroll saw)
- Phillips screwdriver
- Scroll saw
- Hammer
- Tape measure
- Square
- Awl
- Pencil
- Scissors
- Compass
- Sandpaper
- Thin wire
- Pliers (for hook screws)

# FIREBALLS

Let's fight fire with fire, as the saying goes. The dragon will be mightily surprised when we launch an attack of fireballs (Ping-Pong® balls).

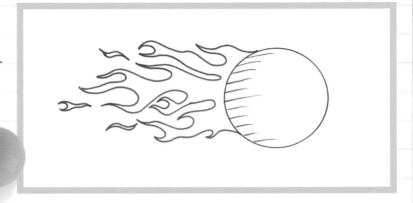

## LAUNCHING FIREBALLS

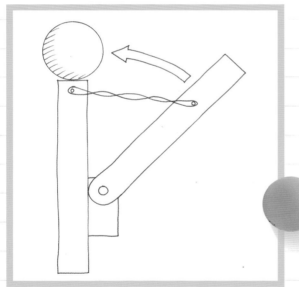

The mechanism for launching fireballs should be like a small Ping-Pong® paddle. This will be powered by rubber bands.

## HOLDING THE FIREBALLS

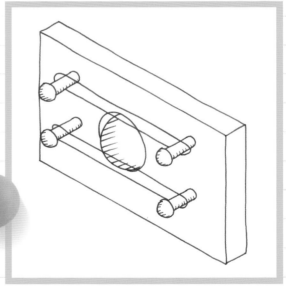

The fireballs need to be held in place so they can be launched upward, downward, or sideways all while we are running, jumping, and dodging. Rubber bands will be positioned to lightly touch the edges of the balls to hold them in place.

# THE SHIELD

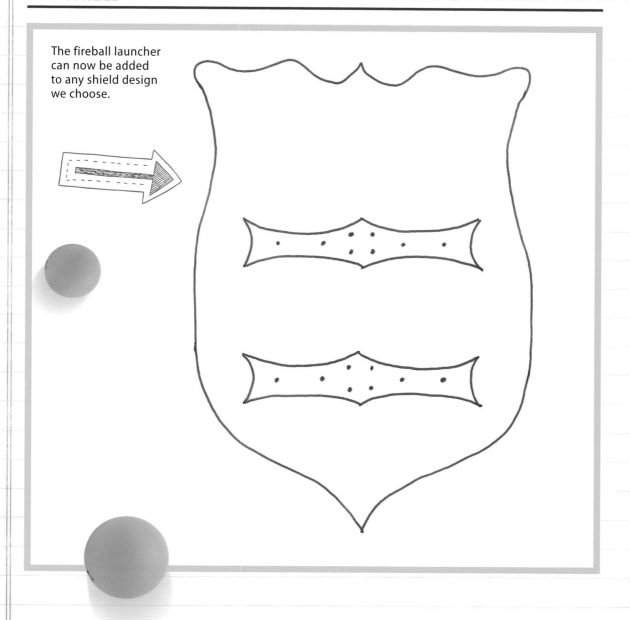

The fireball launcher can now be added to any shield design we choose.

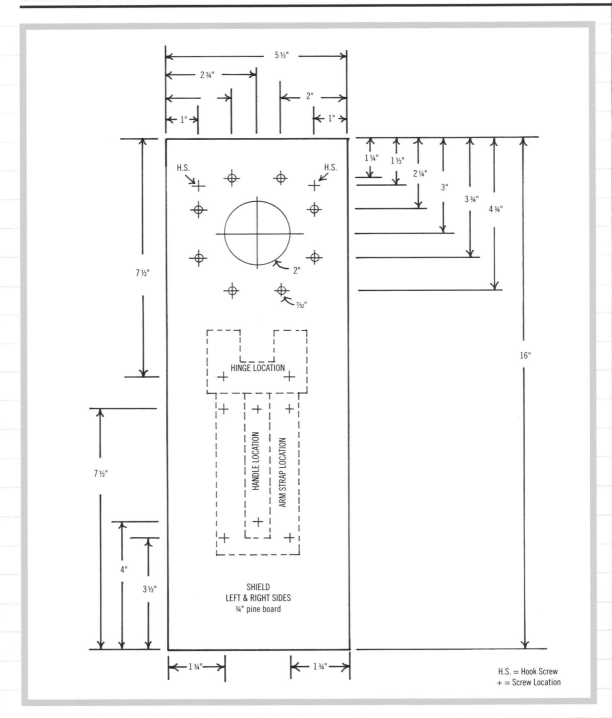

SHIELD
LEFT & RIGHT SIDES
¾" pine board

HINGE LOCATION

HANDLE LOCATION

ARM STRAP LOCATION

H.S. = Hook Screw
+ = Screw Location

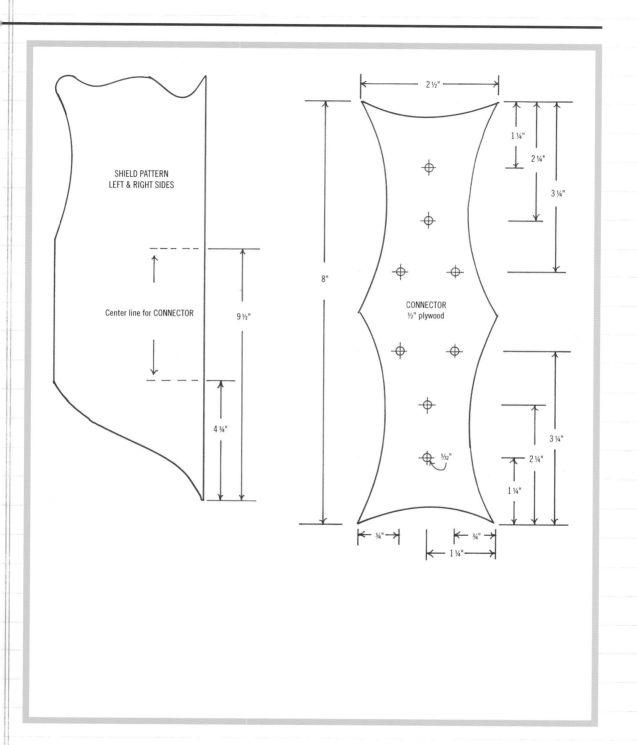

SHIELD PATTERN
LEFT & RIGHT SIDES

Center line for CONNECTOR

9 ½"

4 ¾"

2 ½"

1 ¼"

2 ¼"

3 ¼"

8"

CONNECTOR
½" plywood

5⁄32"

3 ¼"

2 ¼"

1 ¼"

¾"

¾"

1 ¼"

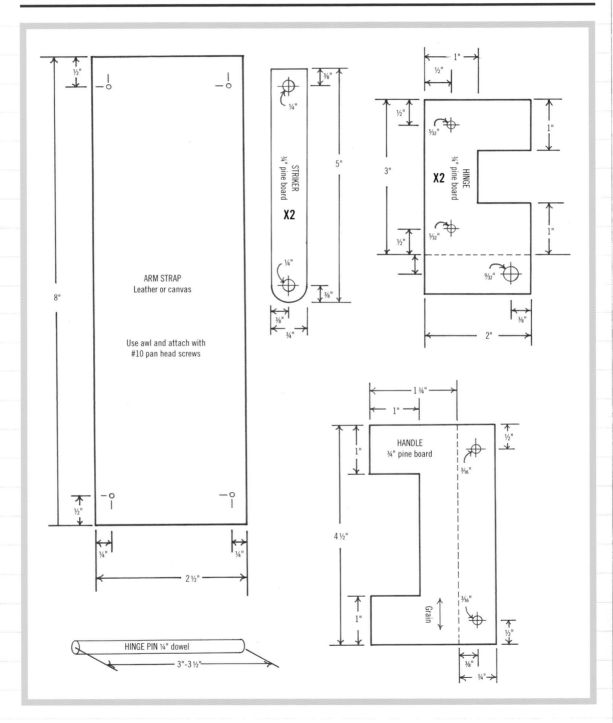

ARM STRAP
Leather or canvas

Use awl and attach with
#10 pan head screws

8"

½"

½"

¼"

¼"

2½"

STRIKER
¾" pine board

X2

5"

⅜"

¼"

¼"

⅜"

⅜"

¾"

HINGE
¾" pine board

X2

1"

½"

½"

⅝₃₂"

⅝₃₂"

9/32"

½"

3"

1"

1"

1"

⅜"

2"

HANDLE
¾" pine board

1¾"

1"

1"

½"

3/16"

4½"

1"

Grain

3/16"

½"

⅜"

¾"

HINGE PIN ¼" dowel

3"–3½"

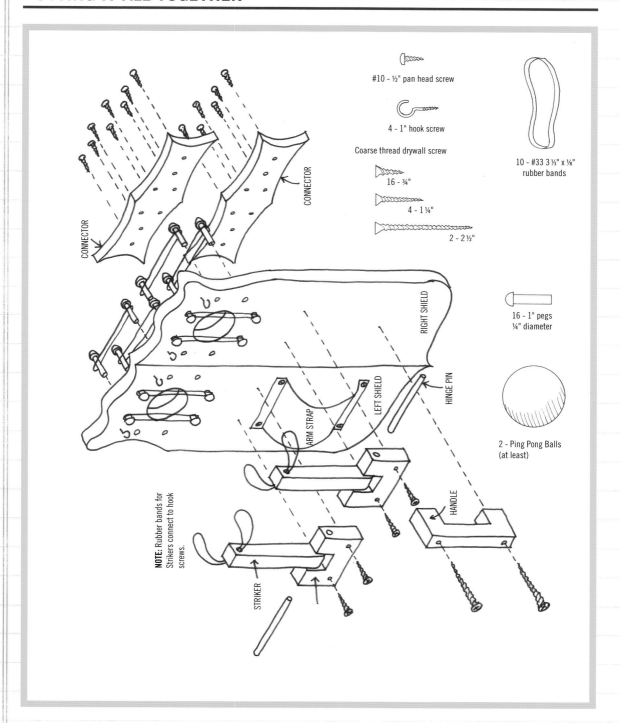

#10 - ½" pan head screw

4 - 1" hook screw

Coarse thread drywall screw

16 - ¾"

4 - 1¼"

2 - 2½"

10 - #33 3⅓" x ⅛"
rubber bands

16 - 1" pegs
¼" diameter

2 - Ping Pong Balls
(at least)

CONNECTOR

CONNECTOR

RIGHT SHIELD

LEFT SHIELD

HINGE PIN

ARM STRAP

HANDLE

STRIKER

**NOTE:** Rubber bands for Strikers connect to hook screws.

# WORLD'S SMALLEST WOODEN TOY

## Or Totally Useless, Yet Very Curious, Little Jumping Widget

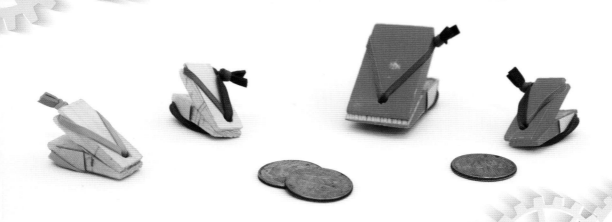

**A**s simple as it is, this toy may captivate you for hours. Perhaps it's the standing backflip and varied landings that fascinate you. Maybe it's the delayed jump that makes you think you have created a living object with a will of its own—a real Franken-Toy. Possibly you are thinking about different designs to make it jump higher or different games you can play. Whatever the spellbinding reason, it will be worth the few minutes of effort to make one (or 10) of these.

## MATERIALS

- ¾" x ¾" x 3"
  (2cm x 2cm x 7.5cm) pine board
- #16, 2 ½" x ¹⁄₁₆"
  (6cm x 1.5mm) rubber band
- Double-sided tape
- Regular tape

## TOOLS

- Drill with bit: ⅛" (3mm)
- Scroll saw
- Tape measure
- Square
- Pencil
- Sandpaper
- Thin wire to pull rubber band
  through small holes

# INSPIRATION POPS UP

Inspiration can come from random events—in this case, it was a small piece of paper that did a little jump on my desk. A little investigation found that it was an L-shaped scrap with a tacky adhesive inside. I pushed the two sides together and watched. Several seconds went by—tick, tock, tick, tock—and then the glue released, the paper unfolded, and the scrap paper did a little hop. Awesome! I had to try to make one myself. The happy little hopper only had 3 components: a spring, a hinge, and sticky stuff—shouldn't be too hard to duplicate

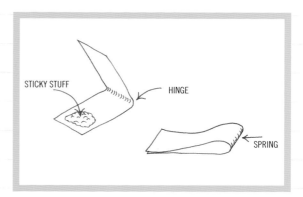

## SPRING

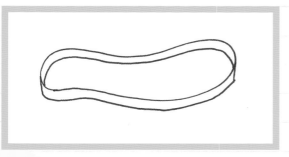

This just needs to be something that "springs" back to its original form. Sounds a lot like a rubber band, and those are easy to find.

## HINGE

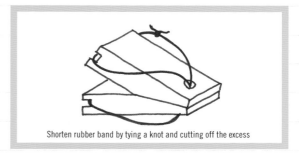

Shorten rubber band by tying a knot and cutting off the excess

Most hinges are held together with a pin. That will be too bulky for this little toy. Instead of a pin, this tiny hinge will be held together by the rubber band. (Shorten the rubber band by tying a knot and cutting off the excess.)

## ADHESIVE

This toy needs an adhesive that doesn't dry out, so normal woodworking glue is out of the question. Double-sided tape will work, but the outside surface will need to be covered to prevent it from sticking to the table.

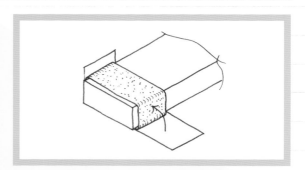

## SAFETY

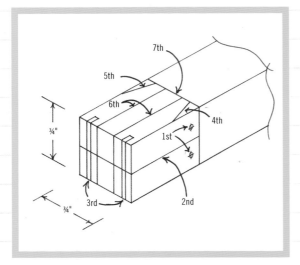

Cutting out small pieces doesn't sound very safe. However, by being clever we can safely drill and make several cuts on a larger board before making the final cut that releases our perfect tiny hinge pieces. Drill and cut the holes and lines in the order shown above on a 3" to 6"-long board to keep your fingers away from the blade.

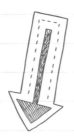

## CREATING THE PARTS

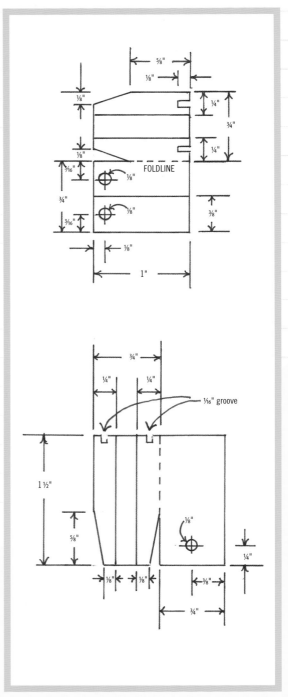

# ICE CUBE DELAY FREAKER

# BANG!

**R**emember the last time you were startled by a loud noise? There was an immediate rush of adrenalin, your heart started pounding, muscles tensed, and your brain tried to determine what just happened. A quick look around perhaps revealed a teary-eyed child holding a limp string surrounded by balloon shrapnel. You breathed a sigh of relief and relaxed again because there was obviously no danger.

The purpose of this mischievous toy is to kick off that same adrenalin rush with a loud POP! And then add some suspense by hiding the source of the noise. The time-delay feature also gives us a running head start in case our prank is not appreciated.

## MATERIALS

- ¾" x 5½" x 14"
  (2cm x 14cm x 36cm) pine board
- ¾" x ¾" x 10 ½"
  (2cm x 2cm x 27cm) pine board
- 8" (20cm) – 14 gauge wire for popper (any thin wire will work)
- 10" (25cm) – 24 gauge wire (heavy wire for trigger)
- 2 – 3" (7.5cm) coarse-thread deck screws
- 2 – 1 ½" (4cm) coarse-thread drywall screws
- 5 – 1" (2.5cm) pegs
- 1 – #64 3 ½" x ¼"
  (9cm x 6mm) rubber band
- 1 – Balloon (or more!)
- 1 – Chunk of ice

## TOOLS

- Drill with bits: ⅛" (3mm), 5⁄32" (4mm), 7⁄32" (5mm), ¼" (6mm), counter sink
- Phillips screwdriver
- Scroll saw
- Hammer
- Tape measure
- Square
- Awl
- Pencil
- Scissors
- Sandpaper
- Pliers
- Wire cutters

## LOUD NOISE

There are plenty of ways to make noise, but the biggest bang for the buck is popping a balloon.

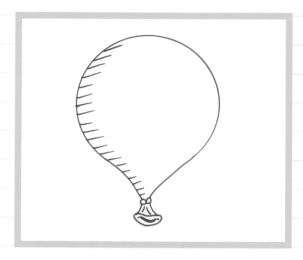

## DELAY

This prank requires a little preparation for us to hide it and then disappear. This means the trigger has to be time delayed. Some ideas for adding a delay:

- Water dripping—might be heard
- A clock—needs power
- Ice melting—Good idea

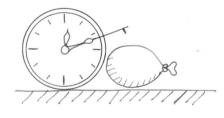

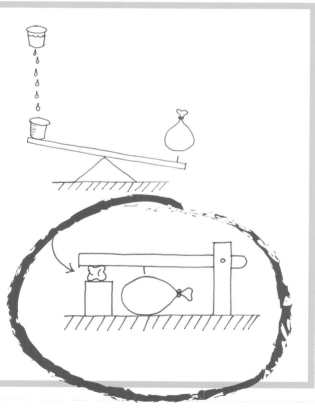

## DELAY MECHANISM

After building a few prototypes, one thing I learned is that ice melts very slowly, too slowly for our devious contraption. The melting process can be sped up by applying a large force such as using a rubber band to pull a thin wire through the ice.

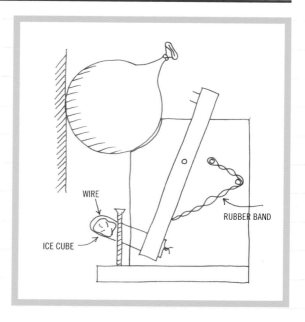

## LOADING

A sharp object will pop the balloon, but we don't want that sharp object spinning around when we are setting this up or testing it out. An extra arm will be added so the balloon popper can be disabled during setup.

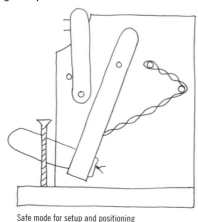

Safe mode for setup and positioning

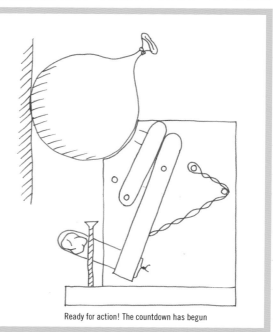

Ready for action! The countdown has begun

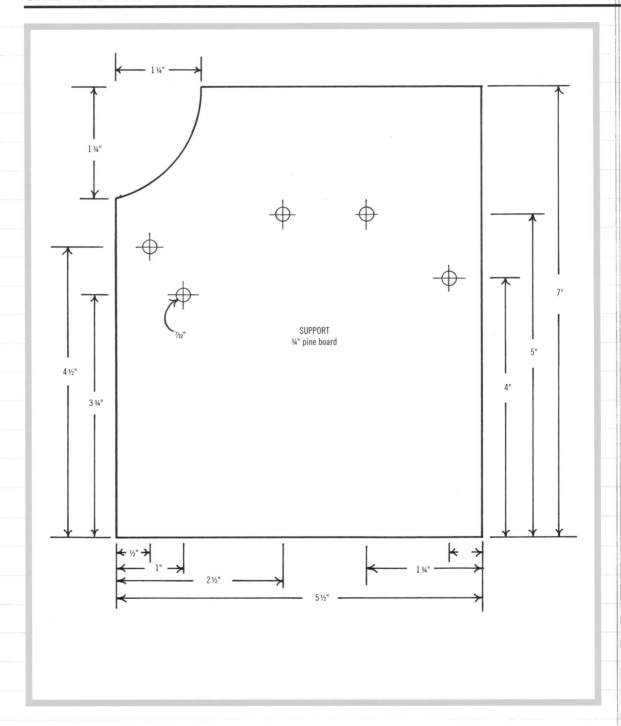

SUPPORT
¾" pine board

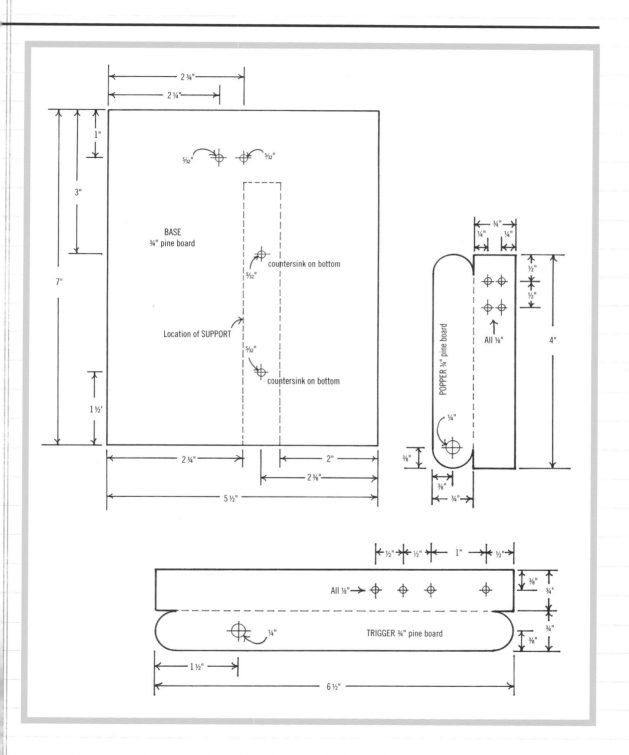

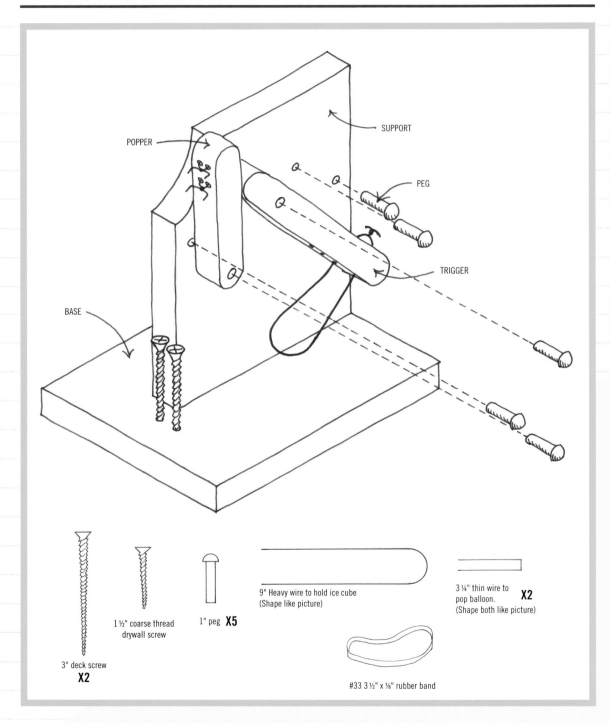

POPPER

SUPPORT

PEG

BASE

TRIGGER

3" deck screw
**X2**

1 ½" coarse thread
drywall screw

1" peg **X5**

9" Heavy wire to hold ice cube
(Shape like picture)

3 ¼" thin wire to
pop balloon.
(Shape both like picture)
**X2**

#33 3 ½" x ⅛" rubber band

Fortunes told! See what the future holds! Gypsies tell fortunes using a crystal ball, but making a glass orb out of wood seems difficult, to say the least. So we will improvise and make our own mystical device—a small box that magically reveals the future. Scan the fortune-teller back and forth over your palm to read and interpret all the creases and lines. Then set it down to see what your future holds.

## MATERIALS

- ¼" x 7" x 6"
  (6mm x 18cm x 15cm)
  plywood or pine board
- ¾" x 1 ½" x 5"
  (2cm x 4cm x 13cm)
  pine board
- ½" x 1 ½" x 10½"
  (13mm x 4cm x 27cm)
  pine board
- ¼" (6mm) dowel, 28" (71cm) long
- 2" x 5 ½" (5cm x 14cm)
  semi-opaque plastic
- Wood glue, hot glue, or sticky
  glue for plastic
- Paper for the fortunes

## TOOLS

- Drill with bit: ¼" (6mm)
- Scroll saw
- Tape measure
- Square
- Awl
- Pencil
- Scissors
- ³⁰⁄₆₀ Right triangle
- Compass
- Permanent marker (for
  marking on plastic)
- Sandpaper

## PALM READER

Our first questions is "what will this thing look like?" We are free to let our imaginations run wild since this has never been done before. Should it be something that you put your hand on like a copy machine, or some contraption that gets passed back and forth over your palm like a little scanner? I like the second idea because it is smaller and more portable.

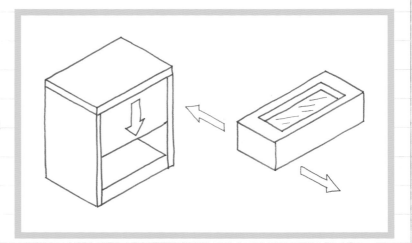

## MAGICALLY APPEARING MESSAGE

We want the box to show a message only after passing over someone's palm. This can be done using the seemingly magical properties of a piece of milky-white, partially translucent plastic such as from a milk jug. Hold this plastic above this page a short distance and you can't read a thing. Amazingly enough however, if you place the plastic directly on the page the words become readable.

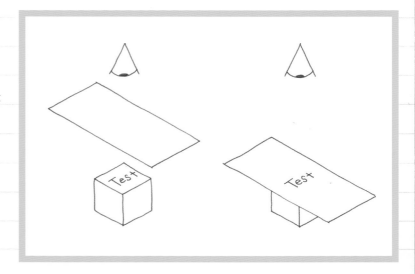

## RANDOM FORTUNES

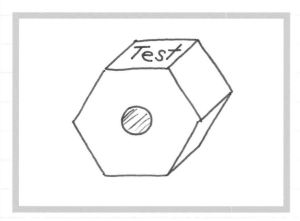

The fortunes will change and be different for everyone who uses the palm reader. The challenge is that the words need to be on a flat surface yet spin around when passed over the palm. A hexagon gives us 6 flat surfaces and can spin around easily. Six hexagons will create a sentence for the fortune.

## THE BIG CHALLENGE

The flat surfaces with the words need to face upwards before being magically revealed. After many complicated tries, I settled on this idea: a hexagon inside a hexagon.

**A. The hexagon can spin on a dowel when passed over someone's palm.**

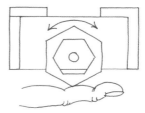

**B. & C. With gravity's help and a little back-and-forth shake, the hexagon will come to rest with one flat side facing the plastic window and one facing the tabletop.**

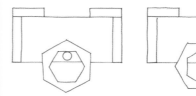

**D. The box can then be set down to reveal the secret fortune.**

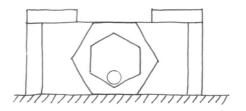

## CREATING THE PARTS

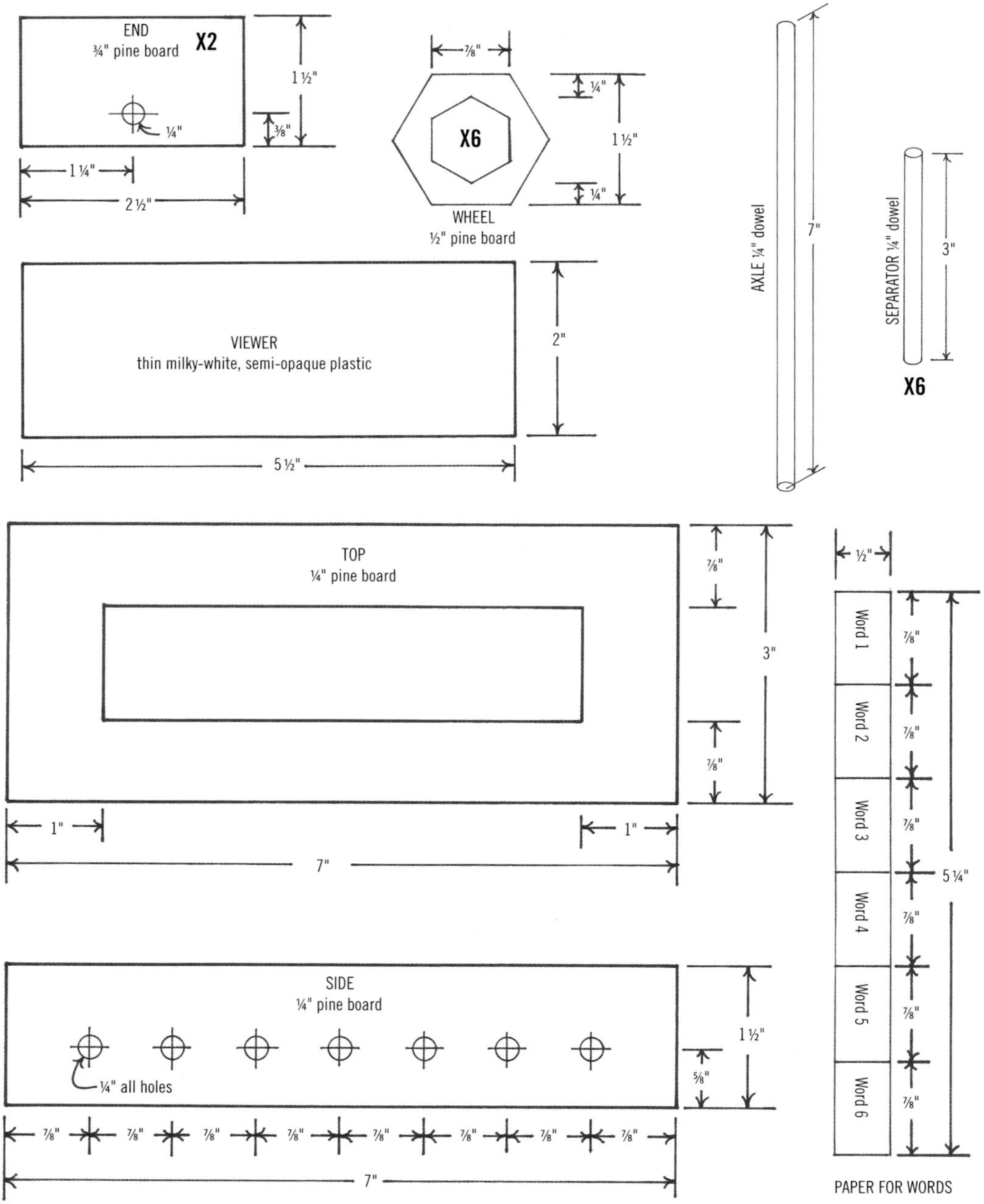

END
¾" pine board
X2
1½"
⅜"
¼"
1¼"
2½"
⅞"
X6
¼"
1½"
¼"
WHEEL
½" pine board
AXLE ¼" dowel
7"
SEPARATOR ¼" dowel
3"
X6
VIEWER
thin milky-white, semi-opaque plastic
2"
5½"
TOP
¼" pine board
⅞"
3"
⅞"
1"
1"
7"
½"
Word 1
Word 2
Word 3
Word 4
Word 5
Word 6
5¼"
SIDE
¼" pine board
¼" all holes
1½"
⅝"
7"
PAPER FOR WORDS


Glue the paper onto the wheels using a glue stick or thin layer of white glue.

# PUTTING IT ALL TOGETHER

I don't usually like using glue because nothing is more boring than watching glue dry. However, this project needed it because the boards are rather thin and might be split using nails or screws.

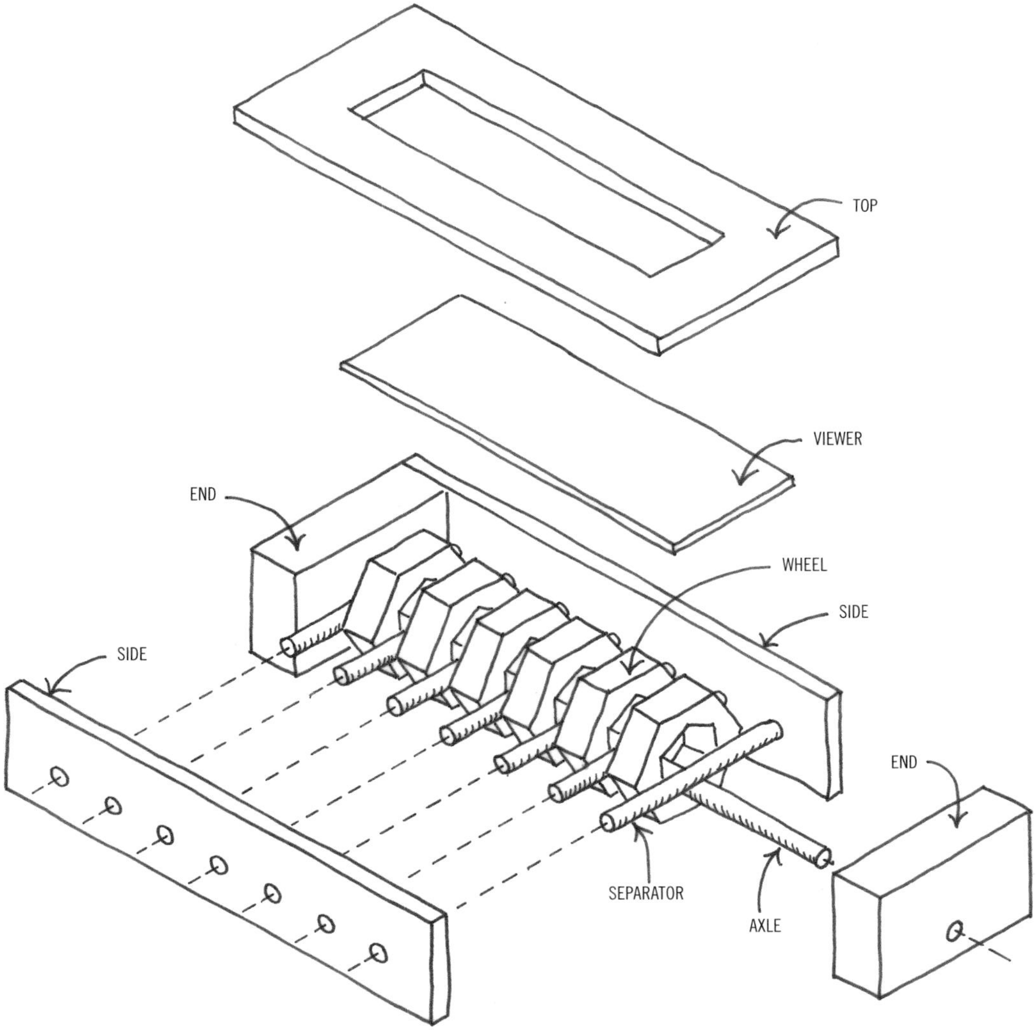

TOP

VIEWER

END

WHEEL

SIDE

SIDE

END

SEPARATOR

AXLE

# WHAT'S YOUR FORTUNE?

Here are some possible word combinations for your fortunes:

Word 1: You, Mom, Dad, Brother, Sister, Friend

Word 2: Will, Won't, Can, Might, Should, Could

Word 3: Eat, Make, See, Smell, Hear, Taste, Touch

Word 4: A, One, The, That, This, Your

Word 5: Large, Slimy, Small, Gross, Flying, Hairy

Word 6: Fortune, Bug, Fame, Monkey, Money, Pizza, Invention

And another set of word combinations:

Word 1: You, A friend, Y'all, Ye, Thou, The brave

Word 2: Will, Can, Should, Shall, Might, Must, Ought to, Could

Word 3: Receive, Win, Make, Create, Share, Eat

Word 4: A great, A small, A huge, An amazing, A smelly, A slimy

Word 5: Treasure, Fortune, Invention, Opportunity, Success, Reward, Present

Word 6: Today, Tomorrow, Repeatedly, Tuesday, In time, Soon, Often, By trying

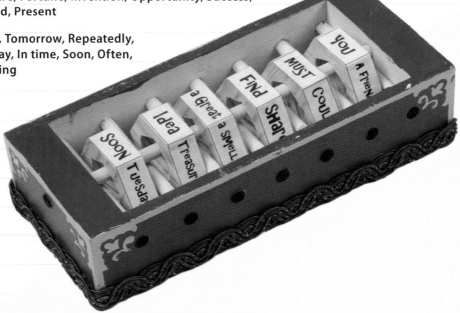

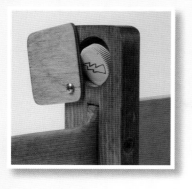

# LIGHTNING SWORD

**BACK TO THE BUSINESS OF SLAYING DRAGONS . . .**

The Fireball Shield is a handy addition to our suit of armor and sword, but what if the dragon is fireproof? He might just give a chuckle and then, with a blast of fire breath, turn my suit of armor into a toaster oven—with me inside! We need a backup plan, something that will really shock the dragon. How about a sword that shoots lightning bolts? Who knows, maybe we'll have a kinder dragon after a few high-voltage jolts. I've always wanted a pet dragon.

Once again I was trying to fling bottle caps through the air. These little discs can have incredible flight patterns. The 2 challenges are to get the bottle cap spinning, and add forward motion.

## MATERIALS

- 1/8" x 2" x 34" (3mm x 5cm x 86cm) plywood
- 3/8" x 2" x 22" (1cm x 5cm x 56cm) plywood
- 3/4" x 2" x 6" (2cm x 5cm x 15cm) pine board
- 1 – 1 1/2" (4cm) coarse-thread drywall screw
- 2 – #6 3/8" (1cm) pan head screws
- Bottle caps (approximately 1/4" [6mm] tall, 1 1/8" [3cm] diameter)
- Glue

## TOOLS

- Drill with bits: 1/8" (3mm), 5/32" (4mm), 1 1/4" (3cm), counter sink
- Phillips and flat screwdrivers to match screws
- Scroll saw
- Tape measure
- Square
- Awl
- Pencil
- Scissors
- Compass
- Sandpaper

## SPINNING

One way to get round things spinning is to roll them down a track. I wasn't sure if this would work to fling bottle caps so I applied the first rule of inventing: Keep It Simple. The first track was just a simple "L" but it worked just good enough to keep the idea afloat.

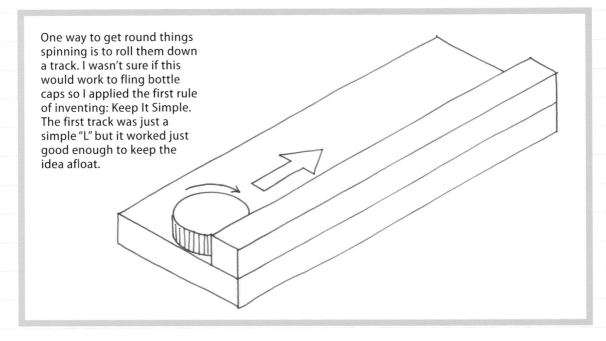

## ENCLOSED TRACK

One problem with the simple "L" track was that the bottle cap flies out before reaching the end. This is fixed by putting a top on the track.

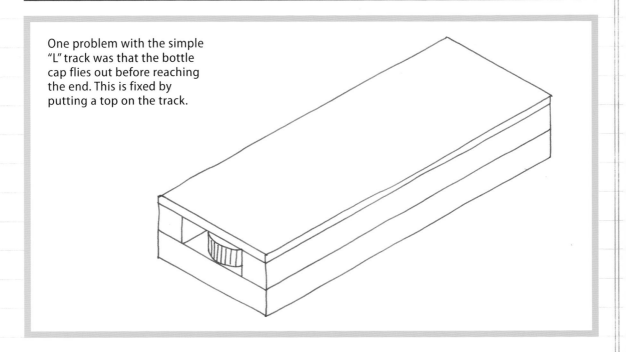

## LOADING

The enclosed track works, but it is still awkward because it has to be held horizontally all the time to prevent the cap from falling out. The solution was to plug the end and add a loading hole.

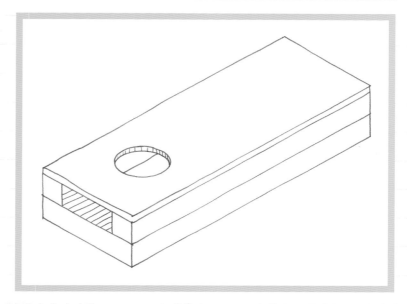

## MAKING IT COOL

Holding the track and flinging bottle caps reminded me of a knight wielding his mighty sword. Just needed to add a handle and cross guard to have the most amazing sword ever. The sword is done, but there is another rule of inventing we can use. It starts with the expression made famous by Steve Jobs, co-founder of Apple Computers, "Oh yea, there's one more thing." So as inventors we must strive to add "one more thing" to an already incredible, one-of-a kind sword. How about secret compartments to hold extra lightning bolts?

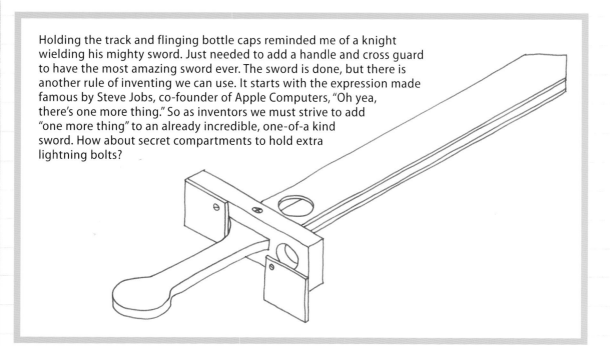

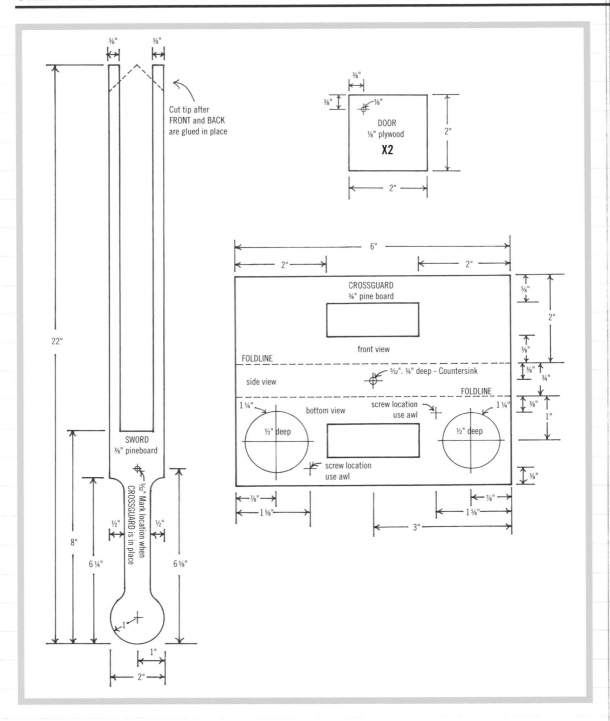

³⁄₈"  ³⁄₈"

Cut tip after
FRONT and BACK
are glued in place

³⁄₈"
³⁄₈"  ⅛"
DOOR
⅛" plywood
**X2**
2"
2"

22"

6"
2"  2"

CROSSGUARD
¾" pine board

front view

⁵⁄₈"
2"
⁵⁄₈"
³⁄₈"
¾"

FOLDLINE

side view  ⁵⁄₃₂". ¾" deep – Countersink

FOLDLINE
³⁄₈"
1"

1 ¼"  screw location
use awl  1 ¼"

SWORD
³⁄₈" pineboard

bottom view

½" deep  ½" deep

⁵⁄₃₂" Mark location when
CROSSGUARD is in place

screw location
use awl

³⁄₈"

½"  ½"

8"

6 ¼"  6 ⅝"

⁷⁄₈"  ⁷⁄₈"
1 ⁵⁄₈"  1 ⁵⁄₈"

3"

1"

1"

2"

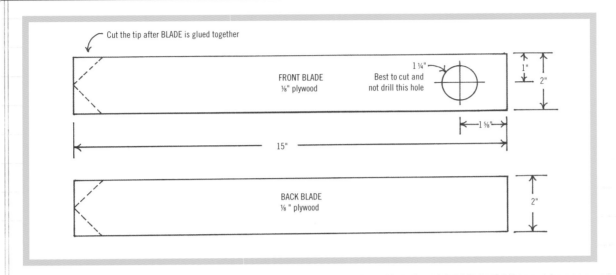

Cut the tip after BLADE is glued together

FRONT BLADE
⅛" plywood

1 ¼"
Best to cut and
not drill this hole

1"
2"

1 ⅝"

15"

BACK BLADE
⅛ " plywood

2"

## PUTTING IT ALL TOGETHER

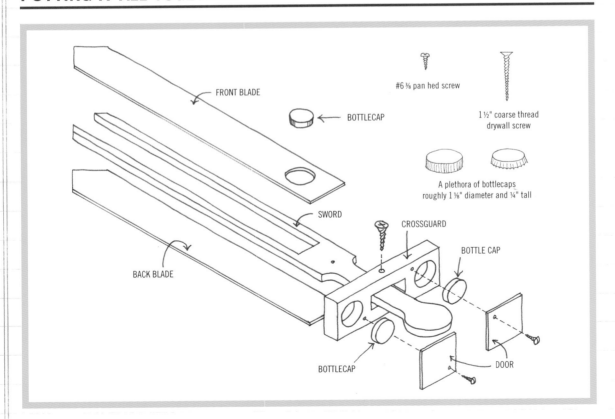

FRONT BLADE

BOTTLECAP

#6 ⅜ pan hed screw

1 ½" coarse thread
drywall screw

A plethora of bottlecaps
roughly 1 ⅛" diameter and ¼" tall

SWORD

CROSSGUARD

BOTTLE CAP

BACK BLADE

BOTTLECAP

DOOR

# GATOR SNAP

This toy has all the fun of bean bag toss with all the danger of gator wrestling. Toss a bean bag fish into the gator's gaping mouth. A direct hit and the gator's jaws snap shut.

The toy was inspired by my son Adam taking a gator wrestling class—in Mosca, Colorado, of all places. Colorado Gators Reptile Park is set on naturally occurring hot springs to keep the gators as happy as gators can be year round. They offer gator wrestling classes to any one brave, or stupid, enough to hop into a pond full of adult alligators. So, after a day of watching and hearing huge jaws snap shut, I wanted to capture that adrenalin rush without the risk of losing my arm.

## MATERIALS

- 2 – ¾" x 5" x 10"
  (2cm x 13cm x 25cm) pine board
- 1 – ¾" x 2 ¼" x 6 ⅜"
  (2cm x 5.5cm x 16cm) pine board
- ¾" x 1 ¾" x 6 ½"
  (2cm x 4.5cm x 16.5cm) pine board
- ¾" x ¾" x 4 ½"
  (2cm x 2cm x 11.5cm) pine board
- 1" (2.5cm) dowel 2 ½" (6cm) long
- ¾" (2cm) dowel 5 ¼" (13cm) long
- ½" (13mm) dowel 16 ½" (42cm) long
- ¼" (6mm) dowel 3 ¼" (8cm) long
- 1 ½" (4cm) wood sphere
- 8 – 1 ¼" (3cm) coarse-thread drywall screws
- 4 – 1" (2.5cm) pegs
- 2 rubber bands
- Glue

## TOOLS

- Drill with bits
  ¾" (2cm), ½" (13mm), 3/16" (4.5mm), 9/32" (7mm), ¼" (6mm), 7/32" (5mm), 1/16" (1.5mm)
- Phillips screwdriver
- Table saw or miter saw
- Scroll saw or coping saw
- Hammer
- Tape measure
- Square
- Compass
- Sandpaper
- Pencil

## JAWS

Gators have big mouths and huge jaws. We will bring this toy to life by making a very large hinge with a ¾" (2cm) diameter hinge pin.

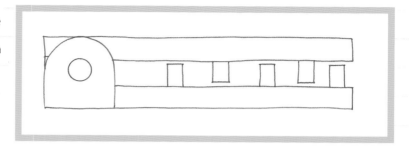

## GAPING MOUTH

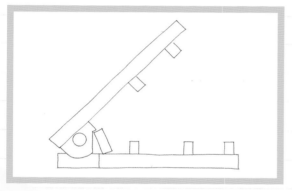

A small block of wood holds the massive jaws open.

## SNAPPING JAWS

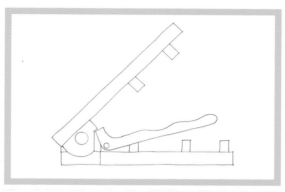

By adding a long lever (or tongue) to the latch, the mouth is easily closed by depressing the lever.

## EXTRA CHOMP

Gravity works great for quickly snapping the gator's mouth, but if we want a real gator-like chomp we need to add some muscle (i.e., rubber bands) to slam the mouth shut.

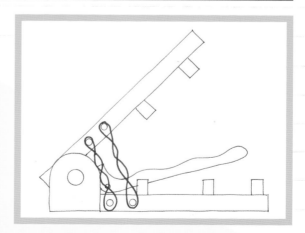

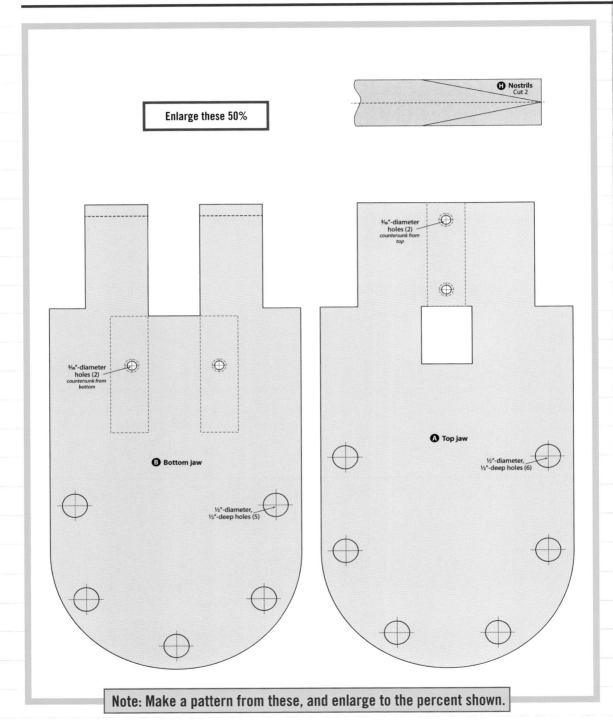

Enlarge these 50%

**H** Nostrils
Cut 2

³⁄₁₆"-diameter holes (2)
*countersunk from top*

³⁄₁₆"-diameter holes (2)
*countersunk from bottom*

**B** Bottom jaw

**A** Top jaw

½"-diameter, ½"-deep holes (6)

½"-diameter, ½"-deep holes (5)

Note: Make a pattern from these, and enlarge to the percent shown.

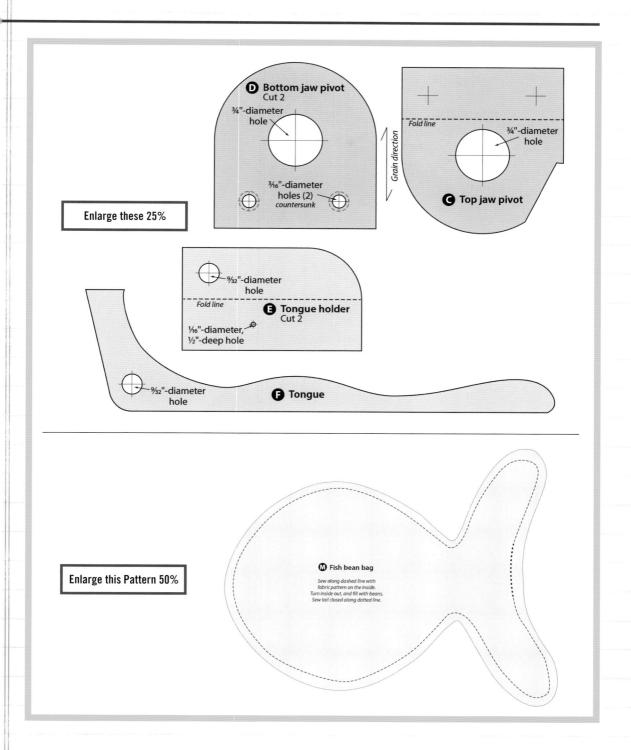

**D Bottom jaw pivot**
Cut 2

¾"-diameter hole

³⁄₁₆"-diameter holes (2)
countersunk

Grain direction

Fold line

¾"-diameter hole

**C Top jaw pivot**

Enlarge these 25%

⁹⁄₃₂"-diameter hole

Fold line

**E Tongue holder**
Cut 2

¹⁄₁₆"-diameter, ½"-deep hole

⁹⁄₃₂"-diameter hole

**F Tongue**

**M Fish bean bag**

Sew along dashed line with
fabric pattern on the inside.
Turn inside out, and fill with beans.
Sew tail closed along dotted line.

Enlarge this Pattern 50%

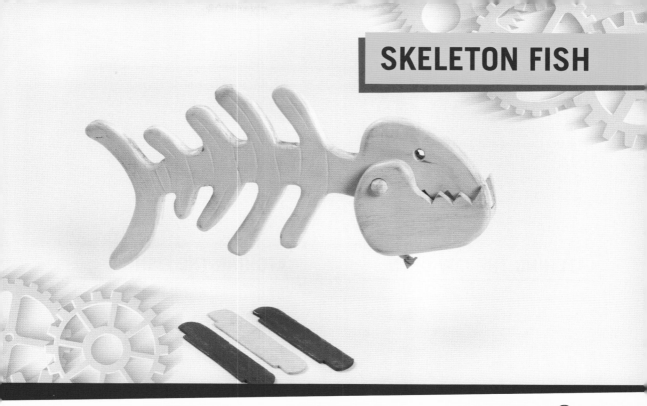

# SKELETON FISH

**B**eneath the sea there lies countless sunken pirate ships with their ghastly, ghostly, skeleton crews still guarding their precious treasures. Stuck at the bottom of the ocean, the lost sailor's only meals come from catching the skeleton fish that swim by. Not enough nourishment to sustain life, but these bony meals are plenty for a skeleton pirate. The fish have razor-sharp teeth and are as vicious and mean as the pirates themselves. Dare we try to catch some for ourselves?

## MATERIALS

- ⅜" x 5 ½" x 9 ¾" (1cm x 14cm x 25cm) plywood
- ¼" x 2 ¼" x 6" (6mm x 5.5cm x 15cm) plywood
- ½" x ¾" x 2 ½" (13mm x 2cm x 6cm) pine board
- ⅜" (1cm) dowel, 1 ½" (4cm) long
- #6, ⅜" (1cm) pan head Phillips screw
- #64, 3 ½" x ¼" (9cm x 6mm) rubber band
- Wide craft stick (approximately ¹⁄₁₆" x ¹¹⁄₁₆" x 5⅞" (1.5mm x 17mm x 15cm)
- #6, 3 ½" (9cm) screw hook
- 3' – 4' (91cm –122cm) string
- Hot glue
- Duct tape

## TOOLS

- Drill with bits: ¹⁄₁₆" (1.5mm), ¼" (6mm), ⅜" (1cm), ⁷⁄₁₆" (11mm)
- Phillips screwdriver
- Scroll saw
- Tape measure
- Square
- Awl
- Pencil
- Scissors
- Sandpaper
- Thin wire

# SNAPPING JAWS

To be as vicious as possible, the fish needs sharp teeth in a huge mouth that can snap shut. We will hinge the jaw and add a rubber band for some biting power.

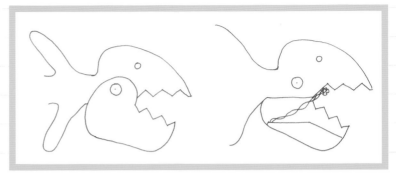

## LATCHING THE JAW OPEN

To keep this as simple as possible, a piece of wood with a small notch will hold the jaws open.

## CATCHING THE FISH

Our fish's mouth is designed to slam shut so the fishhook just needs to dislodge the wooden latch. A large screw hook will be heavy enough to unlatch the jaws when it is carefully dropped into the fish's mouth.

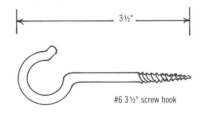

3½"

#6 3½" screw hook

## ATTACH THE FISHING LINE

Tie a series of knots onto the threads of the screw. Run a bead of hot glue over the knots and threads. Cover them with duct tape.

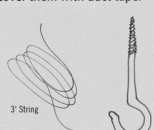

3' String

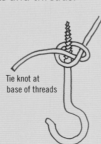

Tie knot at base of threads

Tie more knots to completely cover thread

Hot glue knots then wrap with duct tape

*This now looks like a fishhook and safely covers the sharp end of the screw.*

# CREATING THE PARTS

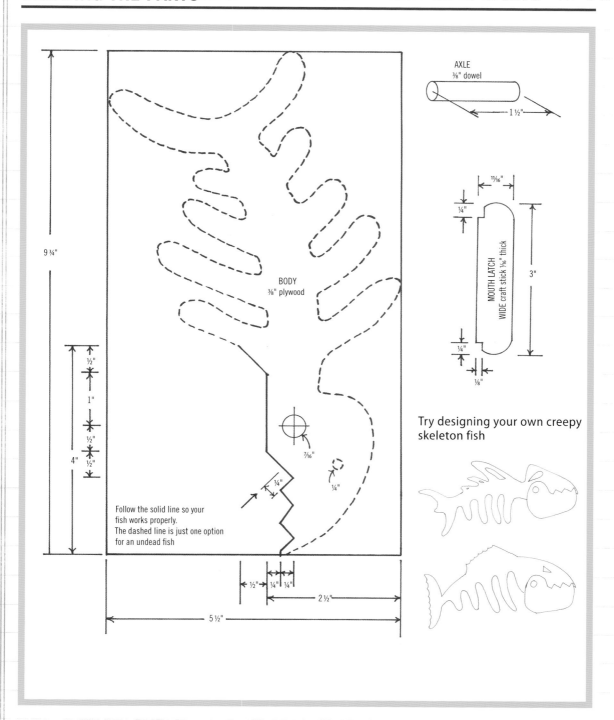

AXLE
⅜" dowel

1½"

9¾"

BODY
⅜" plywood

½"

1"

½"

4"

½"

¼"

¼"

Follow the solid line so your
fish works properly.
The dashed line is just one option
for an undead fish

7⁄16"

½"   ¼"   ¼"

2½"

5½"

11⁄16"

¼"

MOUTH LATCH
WIDE craft stick ¹⁄16" thick

3"

¼"

⅛"

Try designing your own creepy
skeleton fish

# CREATING THE PARTS *(CONTINUED)*

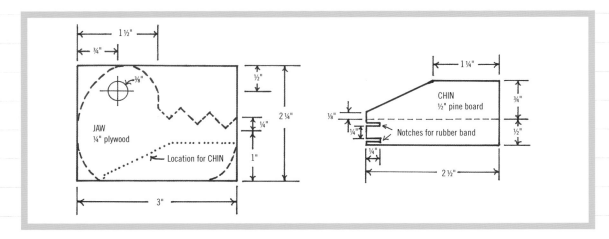

## PUTTING IT ALL TOGETHER

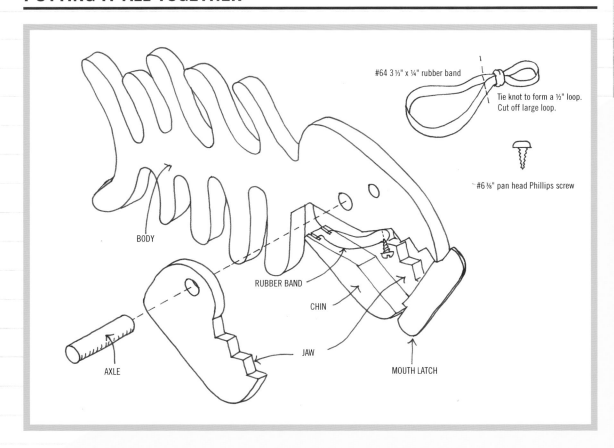

# FISHING POLE
## (Specifically Designed for Skeleton Fish)

Don't even consider trying to catch a skeleton fish by hand. Your fingers are no match for their razor-sharp teeth and bone-crushing jaws. If you like counting to 10 on your fingers, then you'd better design a fishing pole strong enough for these ferocious fish.

## MATERIALS

- 1 ½" x 2" x 2 ¾" (4cm x 5cm x 7cm) pine board (aka, a small chunk of 2 x 4)
- ½" x 1" x 3 ½" (13mm x 2.5cm x 9cm) pine board
- ½" (13mm) dowel, 23" (58cm) long
- 3 – #216 screw eyes
- 6' – 8' (183cm–244cm) nylon string
- Glue
- #6, 3 ½" (9cm) screw hook

## TOOLS

- Drill with bits: ⅛" (3mm), ½" (13mm), ⅝" (1.5cm), 1" (2.5cm)
- Phillips screwdriver
- Scroll saw
- Tape measure
- Awl
- Pencil
- Scissors
- Compass
- Sandpaper
- Pliers

## THE HOOK

We will use the hook shown in the Skeleton Fish project (page 141). This heavy-duty hook won't bend or break in the vise-grip jaws of the skeleton fish, and it is hefty enough to remove the latch when it is carefully lowered into the fish's mouth.

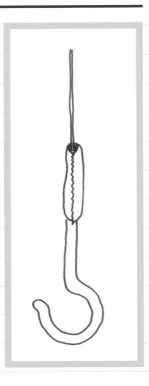

## FISHING LINE

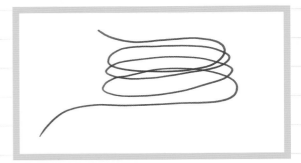

This, too, needs to be very strong. A hefty nylon string will let us hold on as long as we can.

## THE REEL AND POLE

A ½" (13mm) dowel is strong enough to be the heavy-duty pole, and the reel is constructed out of a solid chunk of 2 x 4 for added strength. The simple design of the reel requires only a few holes and a little sawing. Now we can haul in even the toughest skeleton fish in the ocean.

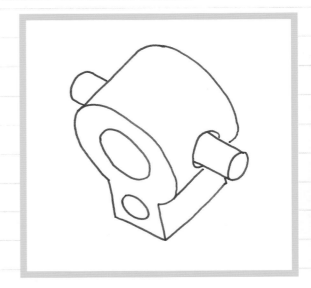

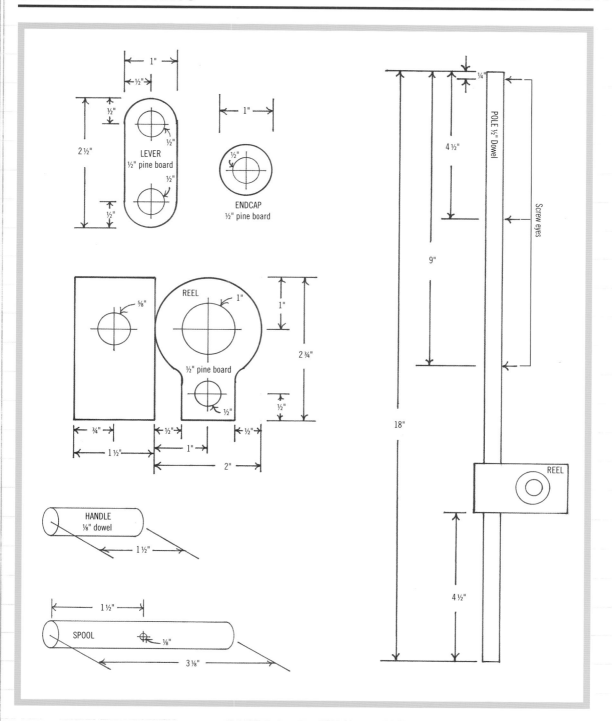

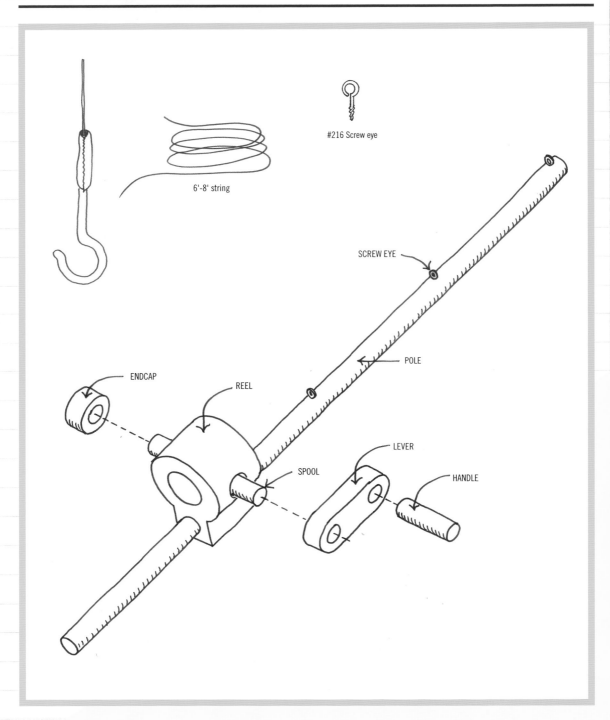

#216 Screw eye

6'-8' string

SCREW EYE

POLE

ENDCAP

REEL

SPOOL

LEVER

HANDLE

# SECRET DRAWER SHELF

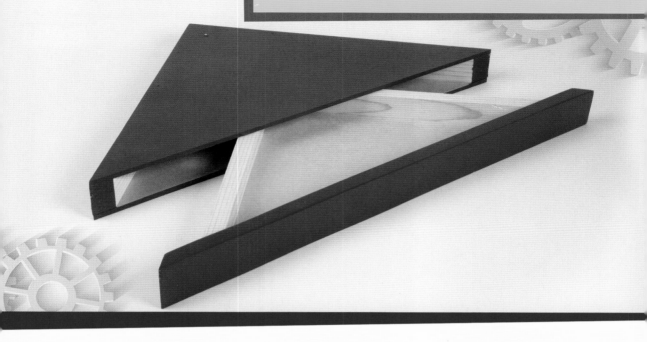

I hope by now you've made some of the projects in this book and have also started making your own inventions. If so, you are probably running out of places to display all your incredible creations. Time to add a shelf to your room. Oh, but not just any old shelf! This shelf is going to proudly display your projects and trophies for the whole world to see, but more importantly, it will keep the top-secret plans for your next invention safe and hidden from spying eyes.

## MATERIALS

- ¼" x16" x 31" (6mm x 41cm x 79cm) plywood or particle board
- ¾" x 2" x 25" (2cm x 5cm x 64cm) pine board
- ¾" x 1 ½" x 32" (2cm x 4cm x 81cm) pine board
- ¾" x 1 ¼" x 28" (2cm x 3cm x 71cm) pine board
- 5 – 1¼" (3cm) coarse-thread drywall screws
- 29 – 3d, 1 ¼" (3cm) finishing nails
- 1 – #17 x 1" (2.5cm) wire nail for lock
- 2 – Hardware for attaching shelf to wall

## TOOLS

- Drill with bits: ³⁄₃₂" (2mm), ⁵⁄₃₂" (4mm), counter sink
- Phillips screwdriver
- Table saw
- Scroll saw
- Miter saw
- Hammer
- Tape measure
- Square
- Pencil
- 45° right triangle
- Sandpaper

## SHELF DESIGN

Look around at a few shelves. Notice that the shelf is actually quite thin, but a faceplate has been added to the front to add strength. We can just hide something behind the faceplate, but it would be very obvious by looking at the shelf sideways. We'll get around this problem by mounting our shelf in a corner.

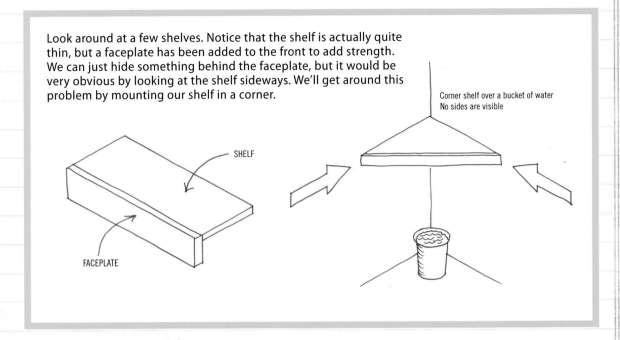

Corner shelf over a bucket of water
No sides are visible

SHELF

FACEPLATE

## HIDDEN DRAWER

Folks naturally assume that the faceplate is just part of the strength and decor for the shelf. We'll trick them by using the faceplate to hide a drawer.

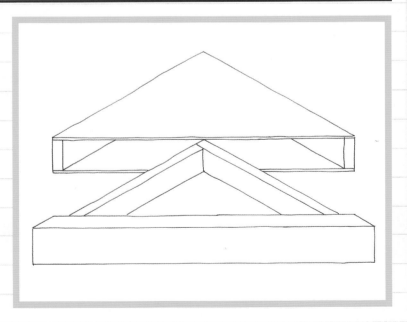

## SECRET LOCK

Drill a small hole through the shelf and into the drawer. A small nail will hardly be noticed, but will keep the drawer locked in place.

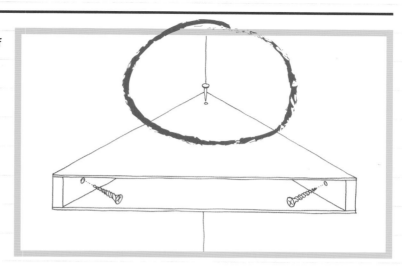

## MOUNTING THE SHELF

Screws attach the shelf to the wall from the inside. Check your hardware store for the best way to mount something on your wall. (I used a 2" [5cm] coarse-thread drywall screw in each side.)

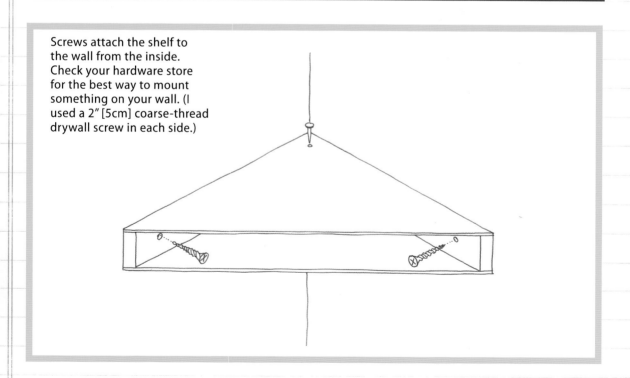

# CREATING THE PARTS

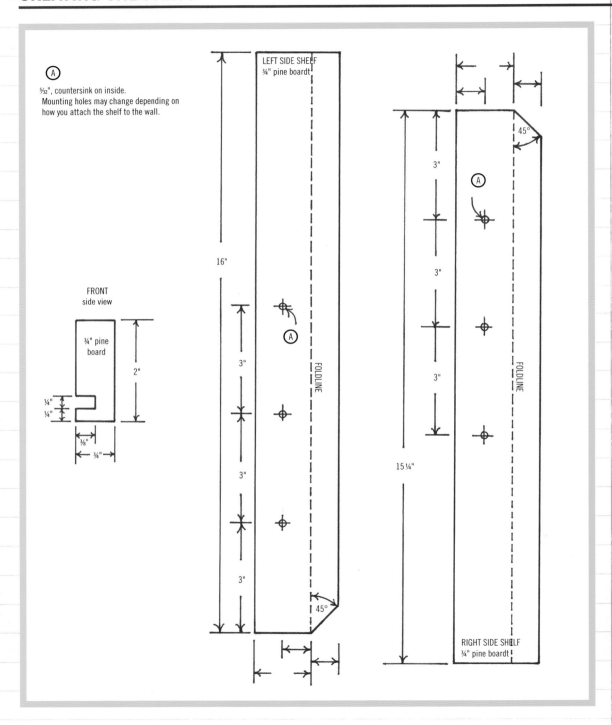

Ⓐ
⁵⁄₃₂", countersink on inside.
Mounting holes may change depending on
how you attach the shelf to the wall.

FRONT
side view

¾" pine
board

2"

¼"
¼"

³⁄₈"
¾"

LEFT SIDE SHELF
¾" pine boardt

16"

3"

Ⓐ

3"

FOLDLINE

3"

3"

45°

45°

3"

Ⓐ

3"

3"

15¼"

FOLDLINE

RIGHT SIDE SHELF
¾" pine boardt

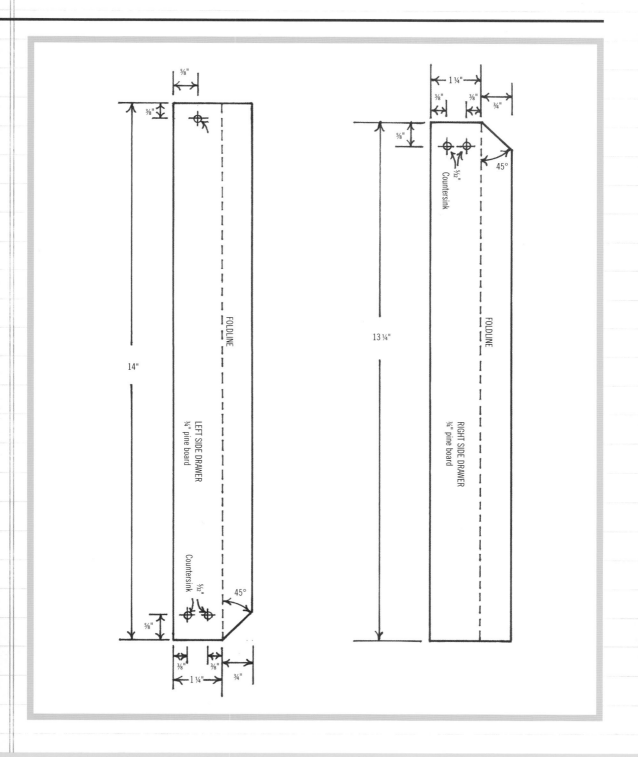

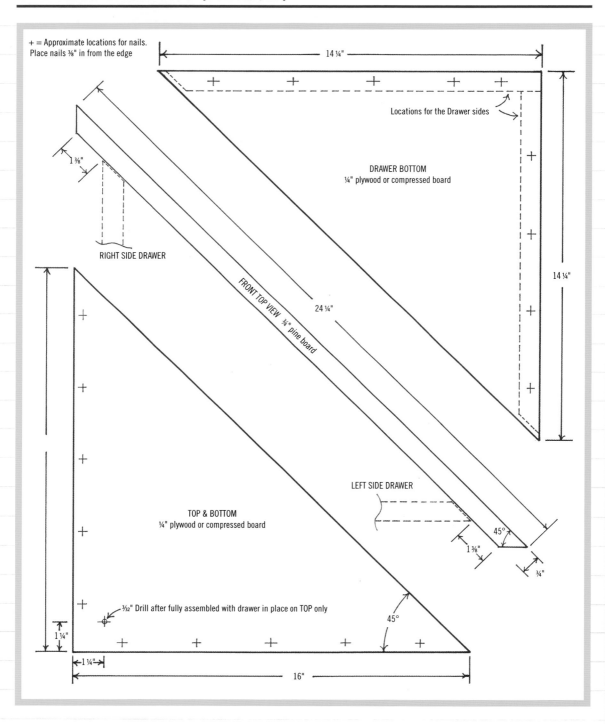

+ = Approximate locations for nails.
Place nails ⅜" in from the edge

14 ¼"

Locations for the Drawer sides

DRAWER BOTTOM
¼" plywood or compressed board

1 ⅜"

RIGHT SIDE DRAWER

FRONT TOP VIEW ¾" pine board

24 ¼"

14 ¼"

LEFT SIDE DRAWER

45°

1 ⅜"

¾"

TOP & BOTTOM
¼" plywood or compressed board

³⁄₃₂" Drill after fully assembled with drawer in place on TOP only

45°

1 ¼"

1 ¼"

16"

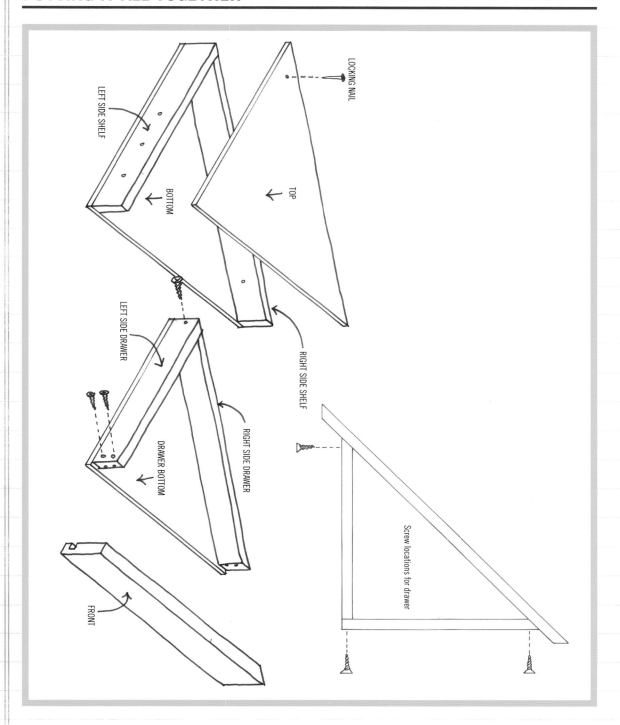

LOCKING NAIL

LEFT SIDE SHELF

BOTTOM

TOP

RIGHT SIDE SHELF

LEFT SIDE DRAWER

RIGHT SIDE DRAWER

DRAWER BOTTOM

FRONT

Screw locations for drawer

# WATER CATAPULT ROOM PROTECTOR

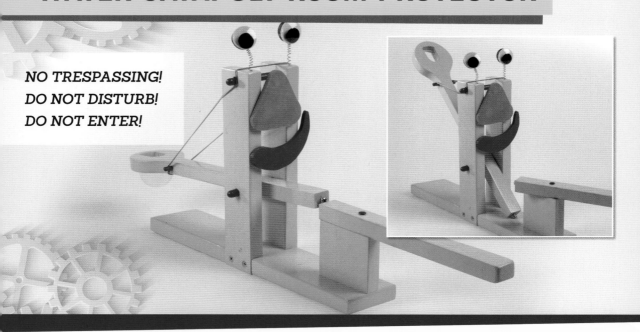

*NO TRESPASSING!*
*DO NOT DISTURB!*
*DO NOT ENTER!*

O kay, you've been warned. A trigger-activated catapult launches a spray of water on anyone who ignores the warnings and opens the door. No harm done by a good soaking, but maybe next time they will think twice about intruding on an inventor's secret laboratory.

## MATERIALS

- ¾" x 3" x 33"
  (2cm x 7.5cm x 84cm) pine board
- ¾" x 1" x 10"
  (2cm x 2.5cm x 25cm) pine board
- ¾" x 2" x 20"
  (2cm x 5cm x 51cm) pine board
- ⅜" (1cm) dowel, 8" (20cm) long
- ¼" (6mm) dowel, 2" (5cm) long
- 2" (5cm) shell from
  vending machine
- 7 – 1⅝" (4cm) coarse-thread
  drywall screws
- 2 – #8, ¾" (2cm) pan head screws
  (Phillips preferred)
- 1 – 7" (18cm) x ⅛" (3mm) rubber
  band or 2 – #64, 3 ½" x ¼"
  (9cm x 6mm) rubber bands

## TOOLS

- Drill with bits:
  ¹⁄₁₆" (1.5mm), ⁵⁄₃₂" (4mm),
  ¼" (6mm), ⅜" (1cm),
  ⁷⁄₁₆" (11mm), 1" (2.5cm),
  2" (5cm) hole cutter
- Phillips screwdriver
- Scroll saw
- Table saw
- Tape measure
- Square
- Pencil
- Scissors

## HOLDING WATER

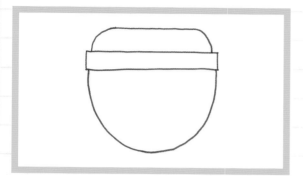

The catapult needs just enough water to make a splash, so to speak. Too much water will be hard to fling, and two little water will not leave a lasting impression on the trespasser. After searching high and low, I found the perfect container—a large plastic capsule from a vending machine (you know the type with a prize in it). The large size was 2" (5cm) diameter that exactly matches a standard hole bit.

## CATAPULTING WATER

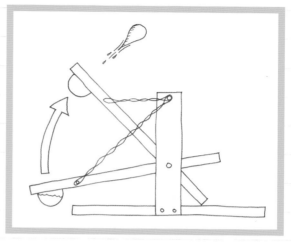

The catapult's arm has to be horizontal so the water doesn't spill. The arm also has to stop at about 45° degrees for maximum fling distance.

## DOOR TRIGGER

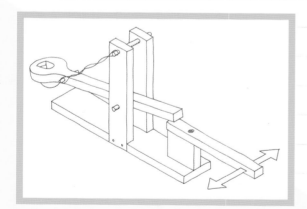

The catapult's job is to drench the intruder when the door is opened. Thus, the door needs to hit a trigger on the catapult.

## HAIR TRIGGER

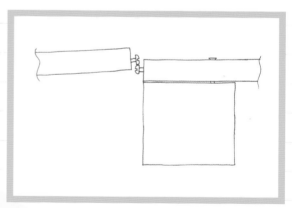

There is a lot of pressure on the trigger so it is very difficult to release. What we need is a very sensitive hair trigger. This is accomplished by carefully balancing 2 screw heads.

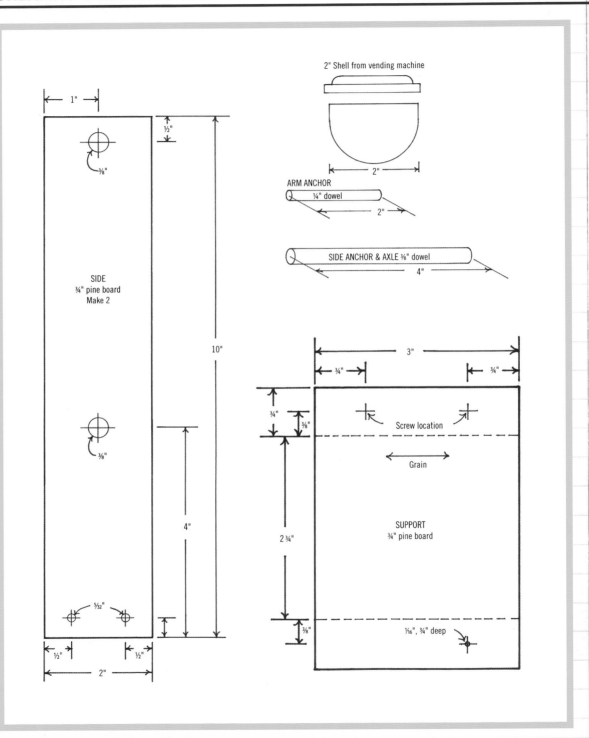

2" Shell from vending machine

2"

ARM ANCHOR

¼" dowel

2"

SIDE ANCHOR & AXLE ⅜" dowel

4"

1"

½"

⅜"

SIDE
¾" pine board
Make 2

10"

⅜"

4"

⁵⁄₃₂"

½"    ½"

2"

3"

¾"    ¾"

¾"    ⅜"

Screw location

Grain

SUPPORT
¾" pine board

2 ¾"

⅜"

1⁄16", ¾" deep

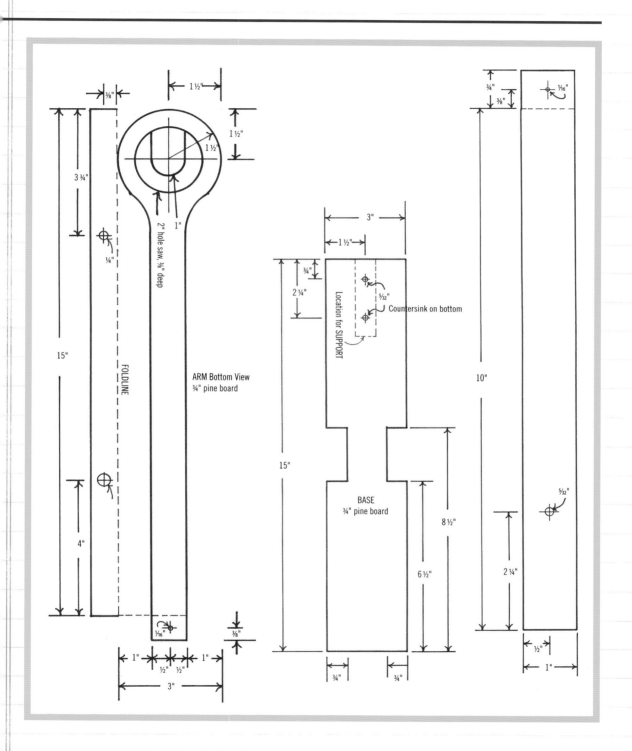

3/8"

1 1/2"

1 1/2"

1 1/2"

3 3/4"

1"

2" hole saw, 3/8" deep

ARM Bottom View
3/4" pine board

15"

1/4"

FOLDLINE

4"

1/16"

3/8"

1"  1"
1/2" 1/2"

3"

3"

1 1/2"

3/4"

2 1/4"

Location for SUPPORT

5/32"

Countersink on bottom

15"

BASE
3/4" pine board

8 1/2"

6 1/2"

3/4"     3/4"

3/4"

3/8"

1/16"

10"

5/32"

2 1/4"

1/2"

1"

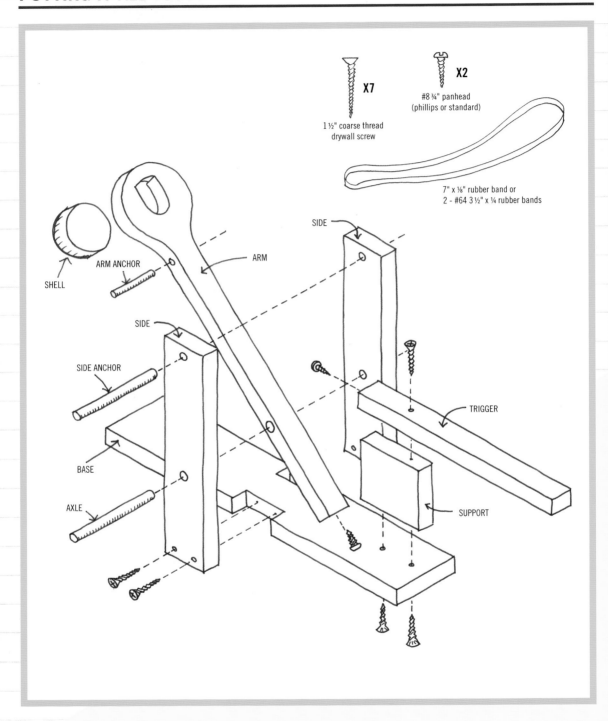

X7

1 ½" coarse thread
drywall screw

X2

#8 ¾" panhead
(phillips or standard)

7" x ⅛" rubber band or
2 - #64 3 ½" x ¼ rubber bands

SIDE

ARM ANCHOR

SHELL

ARM

SIDE

SIDE ANCHOR

TRIGGER

BASE

AXLE

SUPPORT

# ANTIGRAVITY BOX

## MATERIALS

- ¾" x 2 ½" x 7" (2cm x 6cm x 18cm) pine board
- ¼" x 3" x 17" (6mm x 7.5cm 43cm) plywood
- ¾" (2cm) dowel, 2 ½" (6cm) long
- 12 – #6 x ¾" (2cm) flat-head Phillips screws
- 8" (20cm) nylon string
- Graphite or candle (melted wax to lubricate the axle)

## TOOLS

- Drill with bits: ⅛" (3mm), ⁵⁄₃₂" (4mm), ¾" (2cm), ⅞" (22mm)
- Phillips screwdriver
- Scroll saw
- Miter saw
- Tape measure
- Square
- Awl
- Pencil
- Scissors
- Compass
- Sandpaper
- Thin wire
- Glue

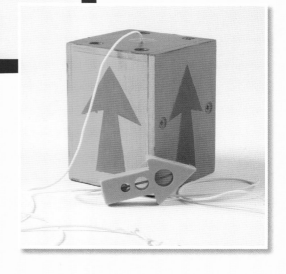

**B**e careful with this toy because you just might blow someone's mind. A simple little contraption, but it is rather perplexing. What you see is a box hanging on a string that passes through the center. Pull the string at the bottom of the box straight down. Be prepared because now it gets weird: the box moves upward! Gravity is a downward force and so is pulling on the string, and yet the box goes up. There must be an alien antigravity device in the box that gets activated when the string is pulled.

**ANTIGRAVITY BOX 161**

## BOX

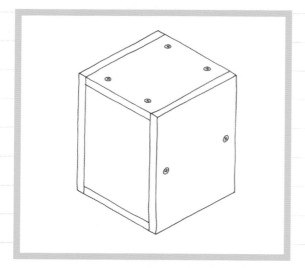

The box should be strong but lightweight, so most of the sides will be ¼" (6mm) plywood.

## STRING

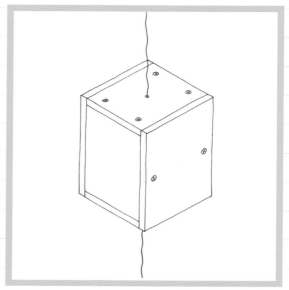

Drill a hole in the center of the top and the bottom, and run a string through the box.

## ANTIGRAVITY

Make contact with a friendly UFO and borrow their antigravity device. (I'm sure they have one because they are far more technologically advanced than we humans.)

## NO UFOS?

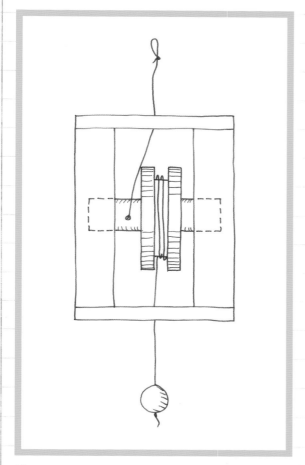

If you can't make contact with a UFO or if they left their antigravity system on their home planet, then try this simple pulley system inside your box.

## SMOOTH RIDE

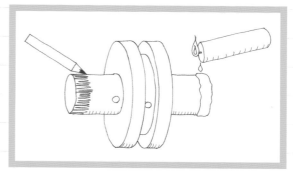

For smoother, quieter movement, reduce the friction between the axle and sides by either rubbing them with graphite from a pencil or melting wax onto them—with adult supervision, of course!

## CREATING THE PARTS

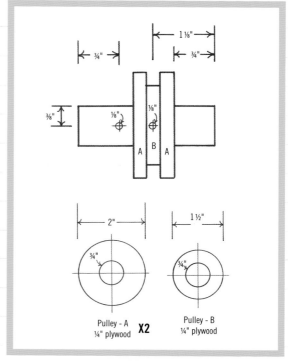

Pulley - A **X2**
¼" plywood

Pulley - B
¼" plywood

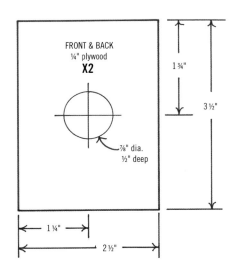

FRONT & BACK
¼" plywood
**X2**

⅞" dia.
½" deep

1 ¾"

3 ½"

1 ¼"

2 ½"

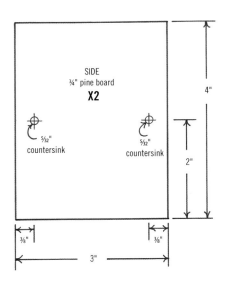

SIDE
¾" pine board
**X2**

4"

⁵⁄₃₂"
countersink

⁵⁄₃₂"
countersink

2"

⅜"

⅜"

3"

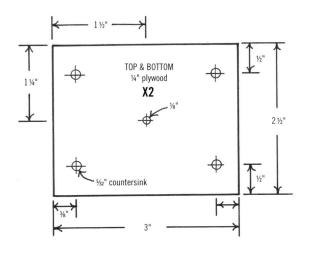

1 ½"

TOP & BOTTOM
¼" plywood
**X2**

1 ¼"

⅛"

½"

2 ½"

½"

⁵⁄₃₂" countersink

⅜"

3"

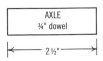

AXLE
¾" dowel

2 ½"

# PUTTING IT ALL TOGETHER

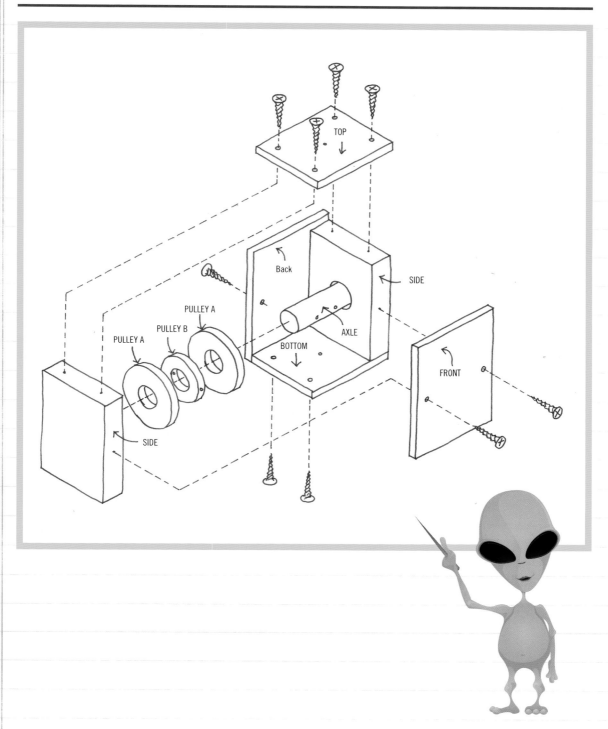

TOP

Back

SIDE

PULLEY A

PULLEY B

PULLEY A

AXLE

BOTTOM

SIDE

FRONT

# WATER BALLOON SNEAK ATTACK

## MATERIALS

- 1 – Wire hanger
- ¾" x 1 ½" x 5" (2cm x 4cm x 13cm) pine board
- 7 – ¾" (2cm) wire nails
- #33, 3 ½" x ⅛" (9cm x 3mm) rubber band
- 20' (610cm) –30' (914cm) strong nylon string
- Lots! – 4" (10cm) water balloons

## TOOLS

- Drill with bit: ⅜" (1cm)
- Scroll saw
- Hammer
- Tape measure
- Square
- Pencil
- Scissors
- Wire cutters
- Pliers

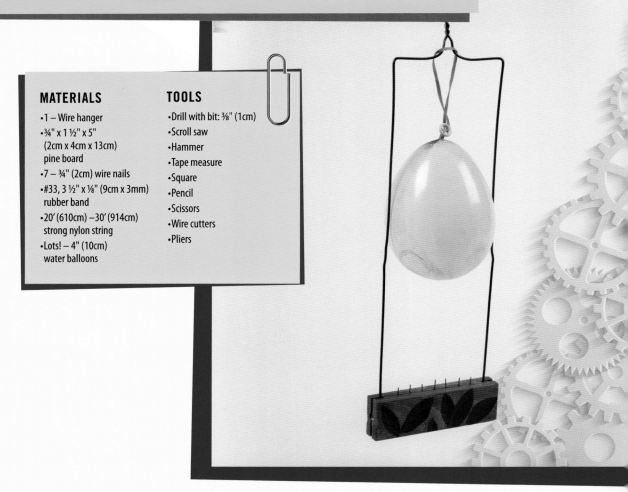

**I**f you're part inventor and part practical joker, then this is the project for you. The mischievous idea: get someone soaking wet when they least expect it. That "someone" should be a person with a sense of humor who will forgive you or a person you can outrun. Choose wisely.

## LEAST EXPECT IT

For this project we're looking for that element of surprise like a huge drop of water falling from the sky on a clear day. Wet, shocked, and puzzled are the feelings we're trying to graciously bestow upon someone. We will plan for a water attack from above.

## HOLDING WATER

Not only do we have to hold the water, it needs to be hoisted into the sky without spilling. A water balloon tied to a string will make this part easy.

## RELEASING THE WATER

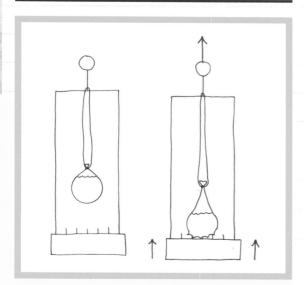

Our only access to the water balloon is the string tied to it. The physics of inertia is harnessed to burst the balloon. The balloon is connected to a rigid frame that has pins at the bottom. The balloon is slowly lifted into place. Then a quick, short pull makes the balloon stretch and hit the pins because the heavy water wants to stay where it is (this is inertia). A cascade of water then falls on our former best friend.

## RUN LIKE MAD

Go! Unless you have a very long string, your soaking wet friend will quickly figure out what just happened and may want to apply the Golden Rule by doing to you what you just did to him.

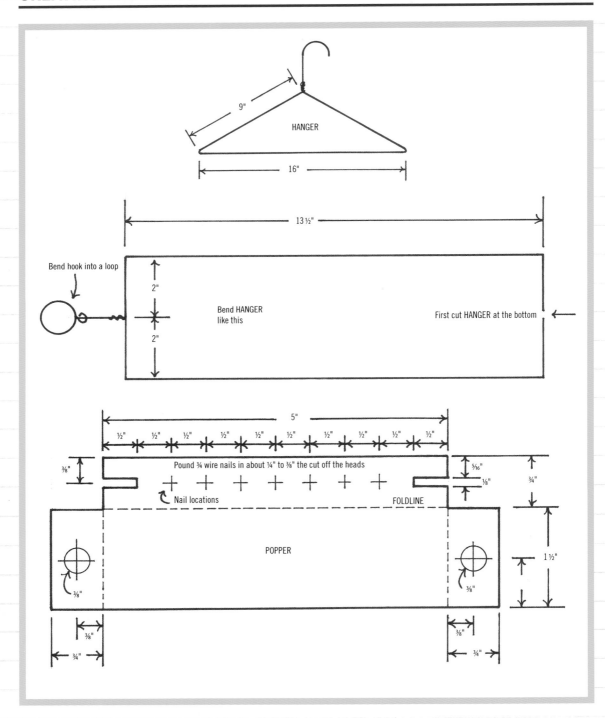

9"

HANGER

16"

13 ½"

Bend hook into a loop

2"

2"

Bend HANGER like this

First cut HANGER at the bottom

5"

½" ½" ½" ½" ½" ½" ½" ½" ½" ½"

⅜"

Pound ¾ wire nails in about ¼" to ⅜" the cut off the heads

5/16"

⅛"

¾"

Nail locations

FOLDLINE

POPPER

1 ½"

⅜"

⅜"

⅜"

⅜"

¾"

¾"

# PUTTING IT ALL TOGETHER

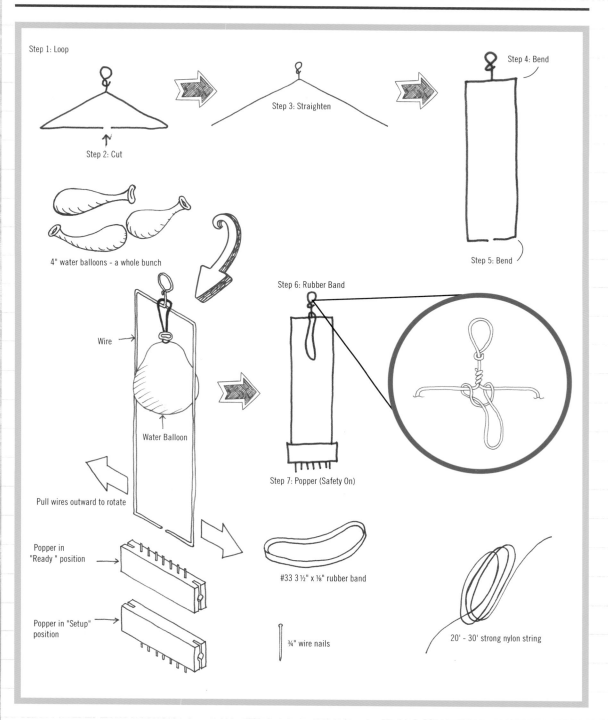

Step 1: Loop

Step 2: Cut

Step 3: Straighten

Step 4: Bend

Step 5: Bend

4" water balloons - a whole bunch

Wire

Water Balloon

Step 6: Rubber Band

Step 7: Popper (Safety On)

Pull wires outward to rotate

Popper in "Ready" position

Popper in "Setup" position

#33 3 ½" x ⅛" rubber band

¾" wire nails

20' - 30' strong nylon string

# HOW TO SET UP

1. Fill a balloon with water. Rotate the wooden piece so the pins are facing downward.

2. Tie the loose end of the string to a stick and toss it over a branch.

3. Pull string until the balloon buster is about chest high.

4. Create a loop in the bottom of the rubber band and insert the stem of the balloon. The balloon should be about 1" (2.5cm) to 2" (5cm) above the wooden piece. You might need to wrap the rubber band around the hanger a few times to shorten it. Once the balloon is in place, rotate the Popper so the nails face upward.

5. Slowly lift the balloon so it is about 2 feet (61cm) below the branch. Tie the string to an inconspicuous anchor.

6. Ask your friend to help you find a precious coin you lost somewhere under the balloon.

7. At just the right time, give the string a short yank to burst the balloon and release a cool and refreshing shower that your friend is sure to appreciate.

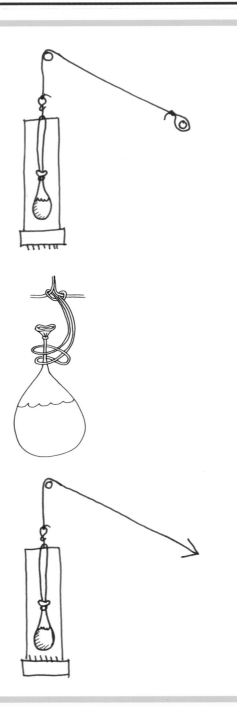

# PIRATE SHIP ROCK TARGET

Shiver me timbers, mateys, there are pirates on the horizon! Seems like we should knock some of those mangy sailors overboard to cool them off a bit. Maybe they won't be quite so ornery after a little saltwater bath.

We don't usually toss our woodworking project into a lake and then throw rocks at it, but that's exactly what this project is all about. The inspiration was simply a stick happily floating in a lake. The fun started when it became a target for the endless pebbles on the beach. With a little imagination the stick was transformed into a pirate ship with a host of ill-tempered, mean pirates aboard and the pebbles became the cannon balls.

## MATERIALS

- 1 ½" x 5 ½" x 14" (4cm x 14cm x 36cm) pine board
- ¾" x 5 ½" x 26" (2cm x 14cm x 66cm) pine board
- ¾" x 1 ½" x 11" (2cm x 4cm x 28cm) pine board
- ¾" x ¾" x 24" (2cm x 2cm x 61cm) pine board
- ¼" x 1 ¼" x 20" (6mm x 3cm x 51cm) pine board
- ⅜" (1cm) dowel, 16" (41cm) long
- ½" (13mm) dowel, 6" (15cm) long
- 8" (20cm) x 9 ¾" (25cm) canvas
- ¾" (2cm) dowel, 12" (30cm) long
- 2 – 2½" (6cm) deck screws
- 8 – 1 ½" (4cm) coarse-thread drywall screws
- 4' (122cm) nylon string
- ¼" (6mm) dowel, 2" (5cm) long
- White and black felt for flags
- 6 – ½" (13mm) screw hooks (I buy #212 screw eyes and use a needle nose pliers to open them into a hook.)
- 5 - #33, 3 ½" x ⅛" (9cm x 3mm) rubber bands
- 3 – ¼" x 1" (6mm x 2.5cm) pegs

## TOOLS

- Drill with bits: ⅛" (3mm), ⁵⁄₃₂" (4mm), ³⁄₁₆" (4.55mm), ⁷⁄₃₂" (5mm), ¼" (6mm), ⁵⁄₁₆" (8mm), ⅜" (1cm), ¾" (2cm), ½" (4cm)
- Phillips screwdriver
- Scroll saw
- Miter saw
- Hammer
- Tape measure
- Square
- Awl
- Pencil
- Scissors
- Compass
- Sandpaper
- Needle and thread or hot glue
- Melted wax

# THE SHIP

Boat building is rather complicated. Our ship needs to float and be stable in the water, which is literally a tricky balancing act. If it floats too much, it tips over. Not enough floatation and it's better described as a submarine. The key to this design is the 1½" (4cm)-thick top deck for stability and the lower layers to add buoyancy.

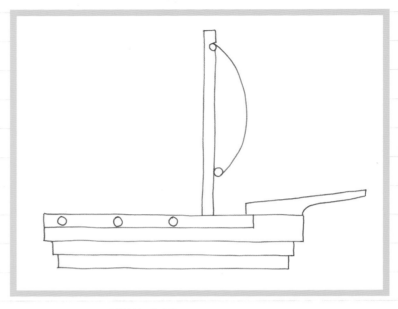

# PIRATES

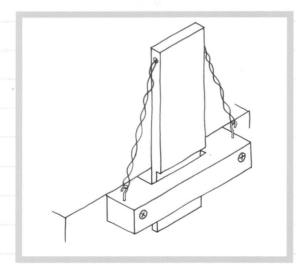

These menacing, scurvy dogs need sea legs to stand on deck when the boat rocks in the waves. A simple latch and rubber band will hold them in place until a pebble plunges them into the salty brine.

# THE SAIL

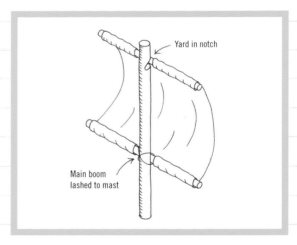

Yard in notch

Main boom lashed to mast

Outrunning the pirates will be easy if their sail can be disabled. The sail's yard (sailor's word for the large dowel that the sail hangs from) will sit in a notch at the top of the mast. The main boom (sailor's word for the dowel that the sail is tied to at the bottom) is lashed to the mast so it doesn't get washed overboard when a well-aimed pebble sends it crashing to the deck.

## RESCUING THE SHIP

Wind and waves have a tendency to move floating objects farther and farther out of reach. Either tie a string to your ship before launching it, or wear a swimsuit so you can get the pirates safely back to shore.

## SURRENDERING

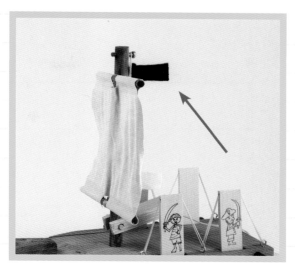

When the pirates have had enough of your pebble attack, they can lower their black pirate flag and raise a white flag to surrender. I've included the plans to do this, but you may skip this step to get your ship onto the open sea faster.

## CREATING YOUR OWN PIRATES

This is how I draw pirates.

This is how my brother Hans draws pirates. He's an artist. Choose your pirates or make your own.

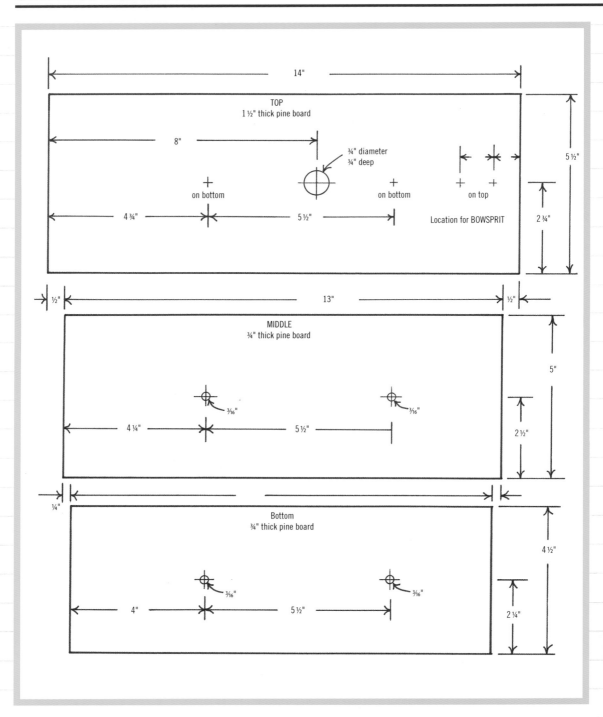

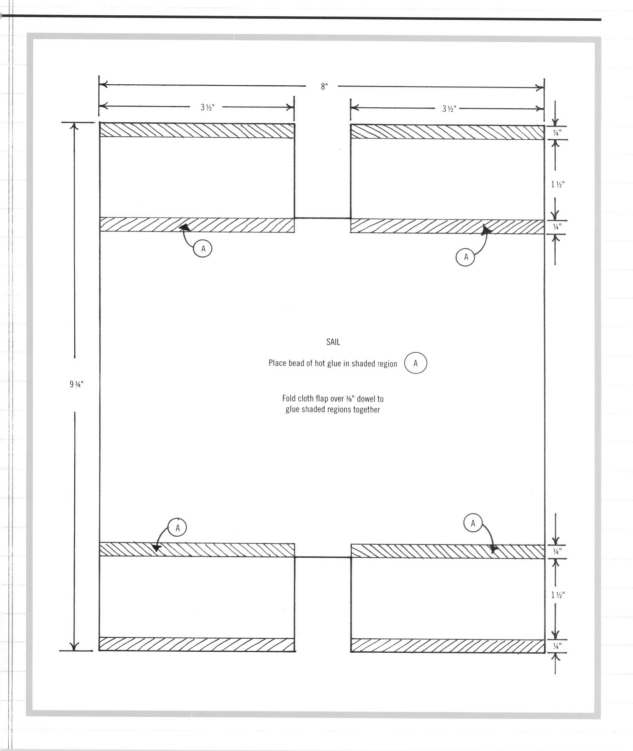

SAIL

Place bead of hot glue in shaded region   A

Fold cloth flap over ⅜" dowel to
glue shaded regions together

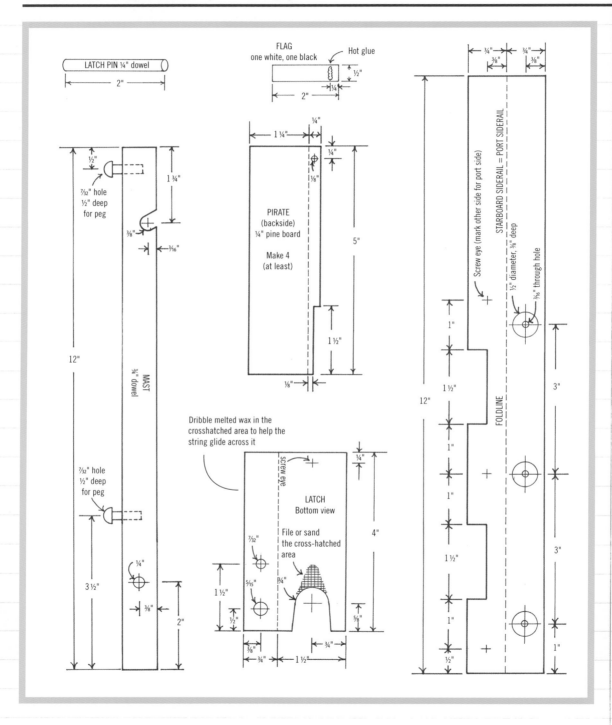

LATCH PIN ¼" dowel

2"

FLAG
one white, one black — Hot glue

½"

2" — ¼"

MAST
¾" dowel

½"

⁷⁄₃₂" hole
½" deep
for peg

1 ¾"

³⁄₈" — ³⁄₁₆"

12"

⁷⁄₃₂" hole
½" deep
for peg

3 ½"

¼"

³⁄₈"

2"

PIRATE
(backside)
¼" pine board

Make 4
(at least)

1 ¼" — ¼"

¼"

⅛"

5"

1 ½"

⅛"

Dribble melted wax in the
crosshatched area to help the
string glide across it

LATCH
Bottom view

screw eye

¼"

4"

File or sand
the cross-hatched
area

⁷⁄₃₂"

⁵⁄₁₅"

³⁄₄"

1 ½"

½"

⅝"

³⁄₈"

³⁄₄"

1 ½"

STARBOARD SIDERAIL = PORT SIDERAIL

Screw eye (mark other side for port side)

½" diameter, ⅞" deep

³⁄₁₆" through hole

FOLDLINE

³⁄₄" — ³⁄₄"
³⁄₈" ³⁄₈"

12"

1"

1 ½"

1"

1"

1 ½"

1"

½"

3"

3"

1"

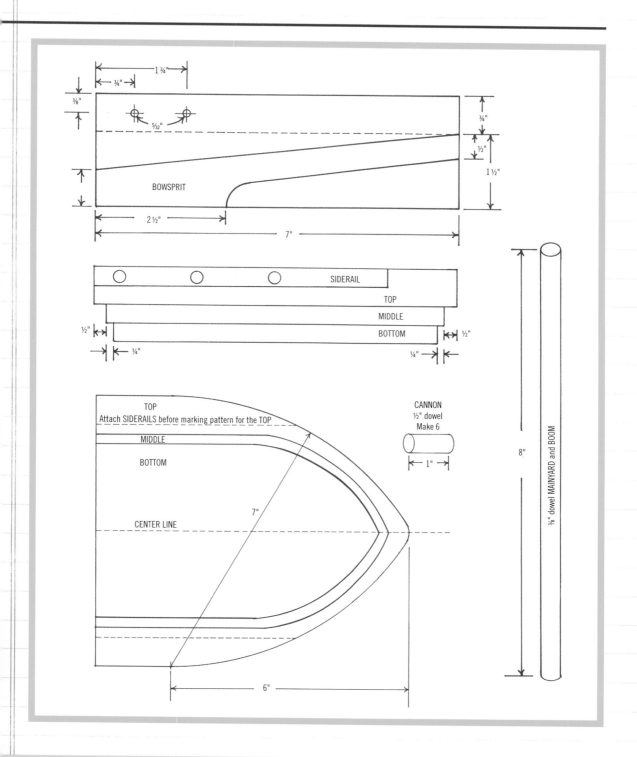

BOWSPRIT

SIDERAIL
TOP
MIDDLE
BOTTOM

TOP
Attach SIDERAILS before marking pattern for the TOP
MIDDLE
BOTTOM

CENTER LINE

CANNON
½" dowel
Make 6

⅜" dowel MAINYARD and BOOM

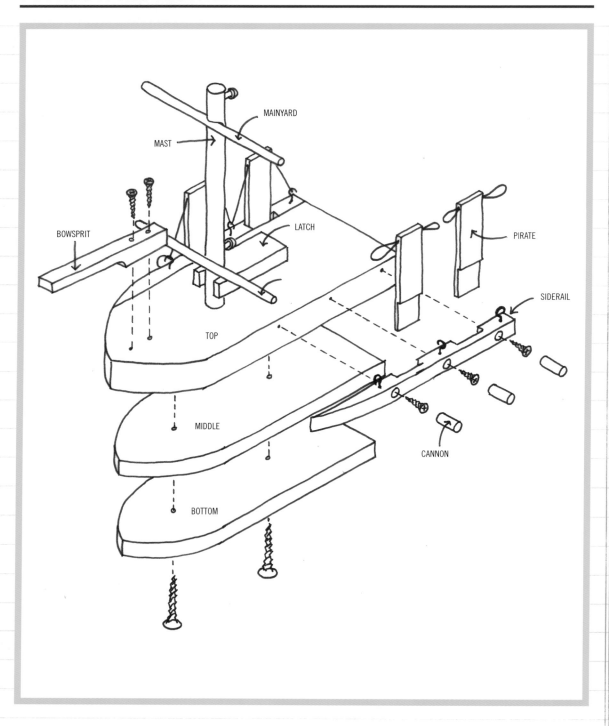

MAINYARD

MAST

BOWSPRIT

LATCH

PIRATE

TOP

SIDERAIL

MIDDLE

CANNON

BOTTOM

# PUTTING IT ALL TOGETHER (*THE PIRATE FLAG*)

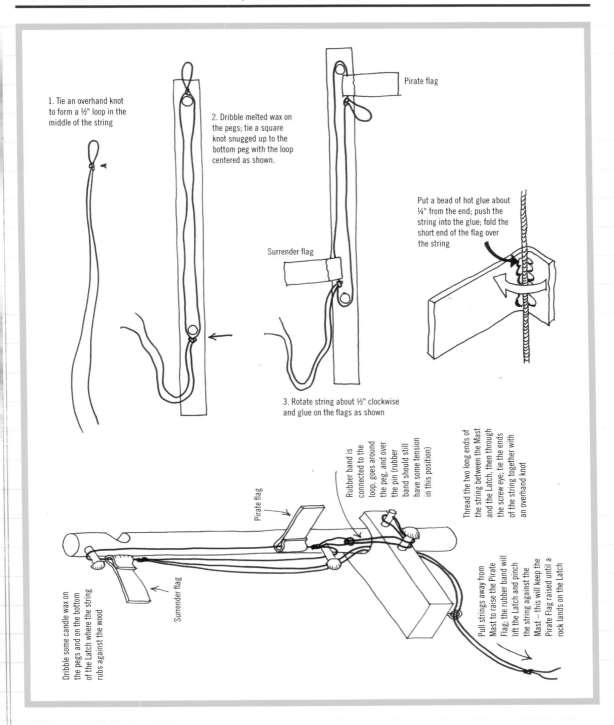

1. Tie an overhand knot to form a ½" loop in the middle of the string

2. Dribble melted wax on the pegs; tie a square knot snugged up to the bottom peg with the loop centered as shown.

Pirate flag

Surrender flag

Put a bead of hot glue about ¼" from the end; push the string into the glue; fold the short end of the flag over the string

3. Rotate string about ½" clockwise and glue on the flags as shown

Rubber band is connected to the loop, goes around the peg, and over the pin (rubber band should still have some tension in this position)

Thread the two long ends of the string between the Mast and the Latch, then through the screw eye; tie the ends of the string together with an overhand knot

Pirate flag

Pull strings away from Mast to raise the Pirate Flag; the rubber band will lift the Latch and pinch the string against the Mast — this will keep the Pirate Flag raised until a rock lands on the Latch

Surrender flag

Dribble some candle wax on the pegs and on the bottom of the Latch where the string rubs against the wood

# COG SLAM

This is the end of the book.

## THE END!

**F**riends are in awe of the creative projects you've made and how you've added your own artistic flair to each one. Woodworking has been added to your long list of talents. With ease and expertise you can drill, cut, and shape wood into moving, functioning contraptions. New inventions and ideas fill the pages of your notebook as you think of ways to make the world a better place. The only thing left to do is clean up your shop and toss out all those oddly shaped scrap pieces from all the projects you've built.

Oh-oh! Here comes that tingly sensation of a new idea forming in your mind. That far-off look comes over your face as you start to envision a game where weird shapes are hit around the floor and slam into each other. Having unique shapes means that each one has a different center of gravity and will move in different and less predictable ways as they ricochet off each other. This will be a very challenging game but tons of fun. Is there time for one more quick project before shop cleanup begins?

## MATERIALS
- 1 ½" x 2" x 3"
  (4cm x 5cm x 7.5cm) pine board
  (just a chunk of 2x4)
- ⅜" (1cm) dowel, 9" (23cm) long
- 2 – 1" (2.5cm) pegs (cut to about
  ½" [13mm] long)
- 2 –#33, 3 ½" x ⅛" (9cm x 3mm)
  rubber band
- All the oddly shaped scrap pieces
  you have.

## TOOLS
- Drill with bits: ⅛" (3mm),
  ⁷⁄₃₂" (5mm), ⁷⁄₁₆" (11mm),
  ¾" (2cm)
- Scroll saw
- Hammer
- Tape measure
- Square
- Awl
- Pencil
- Scissors
- Sandpaper
- Thin wire

## WEIRD SHAPES

Done—just use whatever scraps are lying around.

## SHOOTER

A rubber band, a dowel, and a scrap piece of 2x4 will make a quick and simple shooter.

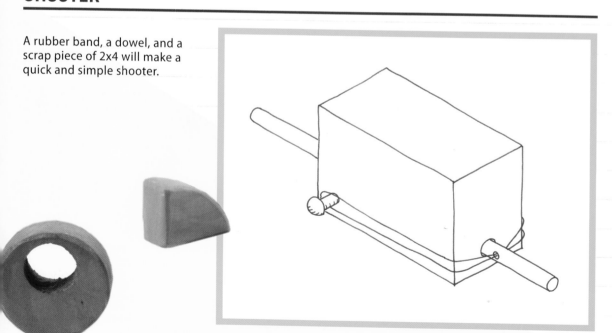

# SHOOTER 2.0

The first version had plenty of power but only lasted a few shots because the rubber band would shear off after hitting the wood block. The fix: don't let the rubber band hit the wood block. Add a notch to the back of the wood block, and wrap a rubber band around the dowel to stop it.

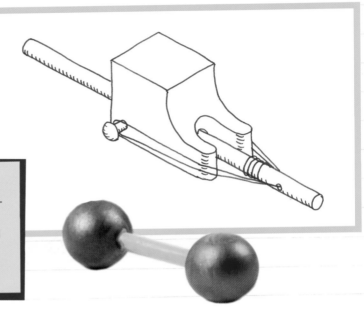

## GAMES

Just start playing around with the weird shapes and eventually a game will pop out.

## CREATING THE PARTS

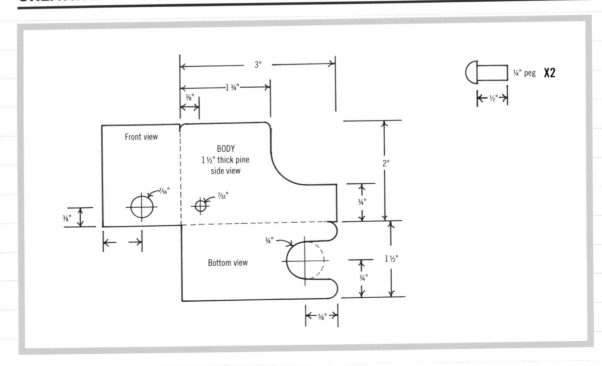

¼" peg **X2**

½"

3"

1 ¾"

⅜"

Front view

BODY
1 ½" thick pine
side view

²⁷₁₆"

⁷⁄₃₂"

⅜"

2"

¾"

Bottom view

¾"

1 ½"

¾"

⅝"

## CREATING THE PARTS *(CONTINUED)*

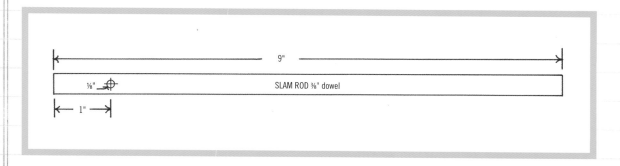

9"

⅛"

SLAM ROD ⅜" dowel

1"

## PUTTING IT ALL TOGETHER

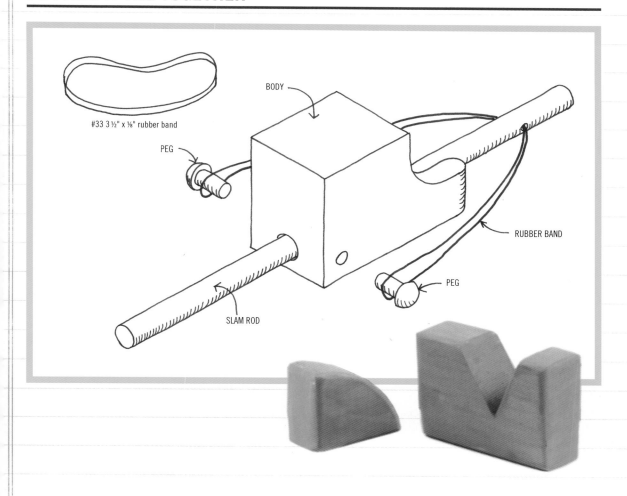

#33 3 ½" x ⅛" rubber band

BODY

PEG

RUBBER BAND

PEG

SLAM ROD

# INDEX